IMPORTED EIGHTEENTH-CENTURY LAW TREATISES IN AMERICAN LIBRARIES 1700–1799

IMPORTED EIGHTEENTH-CENTURY LAW TREATISES IN AMERICAN LIBRARIES 1700-1799

Herbert A. Johnson

THE UNIVERSITY OF TENNESSEE PRESS
KNOXVILLE

Manufactured in the United States of America

Clothbound editions of University of Tennessee Press books are printed on paper designed for an effective life of at least 300 years, and binding materials are chosen for strength and durability.

Library of Congress Cataloging in Publication Data

Johnson, Herbert Alan.
Imported eighteenth-century law treatises in American libraries, 1700–1799.
Includes index.
1. Law—United States—Bibliography.
2. Law—United States—History and criticism.
3. Law—Great Britain—Bibliography. I. Title.
KF1.J6 016.34′00973 78-7368
ISBN 0-87049-220-9

for Barbara

CONTENTS

Introduction	*page ix*
Acknowledgments	*xxvii*
Method, Apparatus, and Abbreviations	*xxix*
List of Libraries and Owners	*xxxix*
Bibliography	*3*
Appendix A: Titles by Category and Frequency of Use	*59*
Appendix B: Law Library Lists	*65*
Index	*89*

ILLUSTRATIONS

Title Page of D'Anvers' *Abridgment*	*facing page xiv*
The Library List of Francis Dana	*xxxv*
Estate Inventory of James Grindlay	*xliii*
Estate Inventory of Library of James Grindlay	*68*
Estate Inventory of Benet Oldham	*85*

INTRODUCTION

Publishers and booksellers have long been mystified by the book acquisition habits of practicing lawyers and judges. As a learned profession the law requires a steady supply of printed materials, yet individual practitioners for the most part have been cautious in the investment of their hard-earned fees in private professional libraries. Law books are generally purchased for utility rather than novelty, and consequently that volume or set which provides the most thorough and concise explanation of the law is the one usually preferred. Beginning with basic collections of English reports and statutes, American lawyers only gradually expanded their library holdings to include treatises imported from the mother country, and in a few cases from Scotland and Europe. The utilitarianism in purchases of treatises helps the legal historian identify those law books that were most influential in the American colonies and states. These works were chosen largely for their practical value as shown by their use in everyday practice. Purchasers may also have been influenced by the collections of mentors and colleagues. The early American practice of lending books to friends doubtless multiplied the influence that any given book may have had, making its interpretations available throughout the community of the owner's professional associates.

Obviously the utility of a book for law practice was not the sole criterion for its acquisition by eighteenth-century American lawyers. Availability of a given title, at the local bookseller or within the reach of a London correspondent, doubtless played an important role in book purchases. Rarity of a title in Britain would lessen the likelihood that it would be sold across the Atlantic. On the other hand the reprinting of useful law books was not infrequent, and a title that enjoyed an active market either at home or in the colonies would normally not be permitted to go out of print.[1] It is also readily apparent that the acquisition of one edition of a title might discourage a would-be purchaser from seeking a revised or corrected edition. These factors are closely interrelated with the practical value of the book in determining the number of titles that appear in colonial libraries or lists of lawyers' books. One cannot say that utility was the sole factor, but on the other hand it seems safe to conclude that utility was sufficiently important to serve as a measure of the impact of a given title on colonial law and practice. In preparing this bibliography the compiler has relied upon the examination of the contents of libraries extant from the eighteenth century, supplemented by the use of library lists and estate inventories of the period. While an effort has been made to include all extant libraries and all libraries subject to re-creation through documentary sources, there are undoubtedly additional holdings that might have been uncovered in the course of a prolonged search.

The user is warned that this bibliography must be considered selective in three major respects. First, it does not purport to include all eighteenth-century libraries. Second, it does not contain a representative library from each of the American colonies and states. Third, it contains only those titles in eighteenth-century American libraries that were, or probably were, published between 1700 and 1799. These limitations are due as much to the current state of eighteenth-century bibliography,

[1]See Eldon R. James, "A List of Treatises Printed in the British Colonies and the American States before 1801," *Harvard Legal Essays* (Cambridge, Mass., 1934), 159–211.

as they are to the limited aims of the compiler. This bibliography has been prepared at a transitional period during which professional bibliographers in Britain and the United States have just begun work upon a short title catalog to eighteenth-century imprints in English. Consequently, it is designed to fill the void that now exists for American legal bibliography of the eighteenth century. Specifically, this bibliography was prepared to identify those law treatises which had the greatest currency in the American colonies and states, with a view toward the eventual preparation of a microform publication of the most common titles.

Despite these restrictions upon the scope and method of this work, it should serve legal historians who seek some convenient guide to the influence of imported law texts upon American law and practice. In a more practical sense it will serve as a reading list for the student who wishes to obtain an eighteenth-century legal education as a foundation for historical research.

At the outset it is important to recognize that case reports formed the backbone of American law libraries. The libraries examined in the course of this survey leave little doubt that the law reports from the Westminster common law courts, as well as the reports of the English High Court of Chancery, were staple reading materials for American lawyers. There is some reason to believe that American reliance upon English reports decreased, and the use of treatises increased, as the American Revolution approached. But however one views the evidence, it is clear that case reports continued in popularity throughout the eighteenth century. Fortunately, all of the reported English cases are available in academic research libraries through the English Reports, Full Reprint. Since the case reports contain materials relating to all fields of law, they are general reference works not identifiable as to subject matter. Consequently, they are not as useful as law treatises in tracing the impact of English and continental law on American courts.

Also included in American law libraries were statutory compilations. English statutes are most prominent in the colonial period, and they are usually supplemented by the appropriate colonial or state statutes—not infrequently some collection of statutes from another mainland colony or one of the British West Indies settlements. This bibliography attests the value of both English and colonial statutes in the practice of American law; several entries pertain to digests of the statutes, abridgements of statutory materials, or special collections of statutes in a particular area of the law.

Although this bibliography contains only a small sampling of eighteenth-century law libraries, it is nevertheless helpful to take a quantitative view of the titles and their frequency of acquisition. In doing so we must be aware that there are significant variations between the separate American colonies and states, and that, in addition, we are dealing with a century that saw substantial change and sophistication in North American law. Rough and vague though our conclusions must be, they nevertheless provide us with some additional insight into the reception of English law and procedure—first into the law library resources of attorneys and judges and subsequently into the law and practice of the American colonies and states. Naturally we cannot be certain that reception into law and practice did not precede the purchase of any given treatise, for lawyers would be encouraged to acquire a title frequently cited by their colleagues and the courts or which treated a field known to be heavily influenced by English law. In short, mere presence of a book in any particular attorney's library tells us little more than that he considered it to be a work that would be of assistance to him in his practice, either to argue for the reception of some English rule or to be better prepared to debate an English principle already engrafted into the law of his colony or state. The occurrence of the title in libraries of other attorneys and judges in the same province, or in collections in other provinces or states, provides some indication of the more widespread reception of English law on the topic of the treatise. Reduced to a minimum, this is all circumstantial evidence that must be used sparingly and in conjunction with detailed study of the statutory materials, court records, and case reports of each jurisdiction before any firm conclusions concerning the transference of English law to American courts can be drawn.

Most popular with American lawyers and judges were works of a general nature, providing an overview of English law and practice. The 43 manuals of practice, almost entirely within the area of common law or chancery procedure, comprise the largest group of titles. Next in number of titles are the more expensive abridgments, frequently multivolumed, covering the law in general (11 titles), the statute law (5 titles), and case law (4 titles). Commentaries or institutes of the law, involving more analysis and discussion than was common in abridgments, are represented by 8 titles. In addition there are 6 titles that may be classified as law dictionaries, 7 as manuals for conveyancing, and 4 as formularies useful in the preparation of writs, indictments, or oaths. These were basic reference works in any working law library, guiding the lawyer to cases reported in his set of reports or to statutes printed or abridged in his collection of English statutes. Furthermore the reference works made available to a lawyer's apprenticed clerks a convenient mode of instruction that might lighten their demands upon the time and patience of their master.[2] Fa-

[2]On eighteenth-century clerkship see Paul M. Hamlin, *Legal Education in Colonial New York* (New York, 1939); L. Kinvin Wroth and Hiller B. Zobel, eds., *Legal Papers of John Adams,* 3 vols. (Cambridge, Mass.,

miliarity with these basic tools of the profession was gained early in a lawyer's career, and preferences for one abridgment over another, or one form book over others, might well have been transmitted through several generations of masters and law clerks. Imported law books continued to find a market in the American colonies and states even after the publication of an American edition of the same title. The one-volume abridgment by Giles Jacob, *Every man his own lawyer,* probably in John Mercer's library well before 1760, was published in New York by Hugh Gaine in 1768 and perhaps in Philadelphia the following year. Yet John McClellan's library assembled after the Revolution contains the Dublin edition of 1776.[3] The most famous law book printed in colonial America was the 1771–72 Philadelphia edition of Sir William Blackstone's *Commentaries*; it was followed in 1790 by Isaiah Thomas's Worcester imprint and in 1799 by an edition published at Boston in partnership with E.T. Andrews. Clearly there was a ready market for American printings of Blackstone's classic, yet both Theophilus Parsons and John McClellan acquired Irish editions that had been printed long after the first American edition appeared.[4] The third general book published in America before 1801 was Baron Redesdale's *A Treatise on the Pleadings in Suits in the Court of Chancery, by English Bill,* published in Philadelphia by Rice and Company in 1789, nine years after its original publication in London. Thomas Jefferson and Theophilus Parsons purchased English or Irish editions prior

1965), I, 1–25; Milton M. Klein, "The Rise of the New York Bar: The Legal Career of William Livingston," *William and Mary Quarterly,* 3rd ser., 15 (1958), 336–37; Herbert A. Johnson, "John Jay: Lawyer in a Time of Transition, 1764–1775," *University of Pennsylvania Law Review,* 124 (1976), 1260–66.

[3]James, "List," *Harvard Legal Essays,* 169, 170; see entry 108 in Bibliography.

[4]James, "List," *Harvard Legal Essays,* 170–74, 185, 206; see entry 13 in Bibliography.

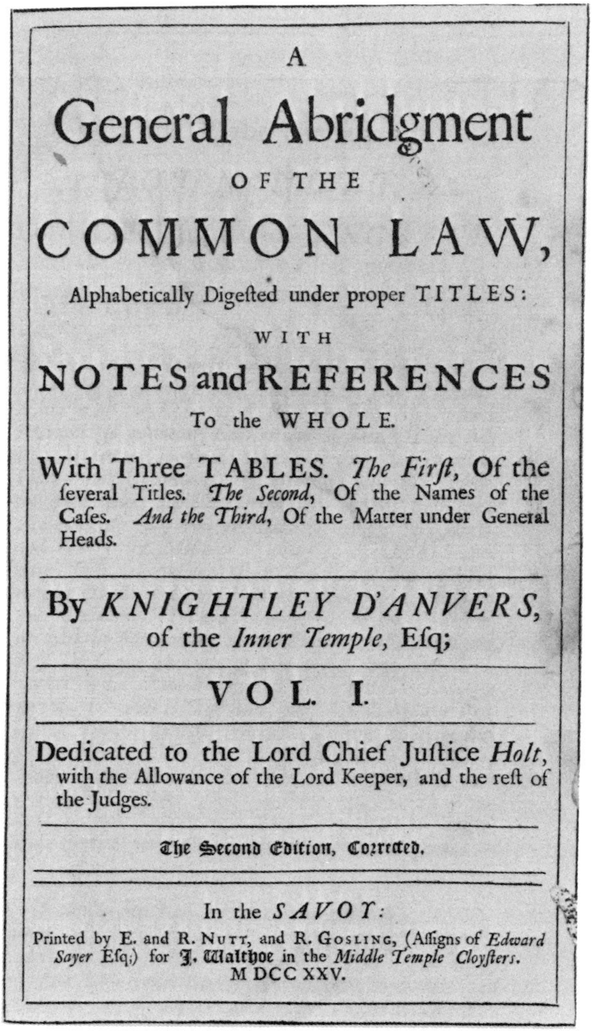

A

General Abridgment

OF THE

COMMON LAW,

Alphabetically Digested under proper TITLES:

WITH

NOTES and REFERENCES

To the WHOLE.

With Three TABLES. *The First*, Of the several Titles. *The Second*, Of the Names of the Cases. *And the Third*, Of the Matter under General Heads.

By *KNIGHTLEY D'ANVERS*, of the *Inner Temple*, Esq;

VOL. I.

Dedicated to the Lord Chief Justice *Holt*, with the Allowance of the Lord Keeper, and the rest of the Judges.

The Second Edition, Corrected.

In the *SAVOY*:

Printed by E. and R. Nutt, and R. Gosling, (Assigns of *Edward Sayer* Esq;) for J. Walthoe in the *Middle Temple Cloysters*.
MDCCXXV.

Title Page of D'Anvers' *Abridgment*, Owned by St. George Tucker.
Tucker-Coleman Collection, Earl Gregg Swem Library, College of William and Mary, Williamsburg, Virginia.

to the American printing, but John McClellan preferred the 1795 Irish edition to the American imprint.[5]

For most of the titles concerning the law in general we may conclude that American publishers were unable or unwilling to compete with English and Irish publishers until the appearance of Blackstone's *Commentaries.* This may have been due to the higher cost of labor in America and the resultant inflation of the cost of printing. On the other hand the quality and quantity of type available in American printshops may have discouraged such ambitious printing enterprises as Charles Viner's abridgment in twenty-four volumes or Matthew Bacon's five-volume work. D'Anvers' widely held two-volume abridgment was certainly within the capability of American publishers, but by the 1760s it may have been considered too antiquarian a title to justify the required investment. Whatever the reasons, it is apparent that the basic reference works in American law libraries before 1800 were printed in England or Ireland. The lack of American imprints in the field of the law in general was due, not to a lack of lawyers in America, as James implies,[6] but rather to the domination of the market by foreign imprints which discouraged American competition. In addition there are considerations of price, quality of the books, and convenience of access to publishers and booksellers, which may have caused a continuing reliance upon imported books to the disadvantage of American imprints. Certainly South Carolinians could obtain their law books as easily from Britain and the Continent as they did from booksellers and publishers in Philadelphia or New York.

On the other hand American authors and printers competed quite successfully with English and Irish publishers in regard to manuals for justices of the peace. Specialized manuals

[5]James, "List," *Harvard Legal Essays,* 184; see entry 170 in Bibliography.

[6]James, "List," *Harvard Legal Essays,* 159.

were published in America designed for use in Virginia, North Carolina, South Carolina, and Massachusetts, and an American abridgment of Richard Burn's manual for justices was also available.[7] A limited number of English or Irish manuals for justices of the peace are in the law libraries surveyed, but it is clear that they did not form a major part of the professional's library. The market for this type of material was probably, as Eldon James suggests, among laymen called upon to conduct the business of the county courts and to serve in the magistracy without the benefit of legal education.

The predominance of the number of common-law practice manuals over that of chancery manuals requires an explanation. We know that colonial and early national law practice was very much involved with debt collection and real property litigation in both areas of common law jurisdiction.[8] In this light the lawyer's buying preferences in the field of common law simply reflect his professional need for form books in those areas comprising the largest segment of his practice. On the other hand, it is important that we take into consideration the place of chancery practice throughout the American jurisdictions in the eighteenth century.[9] Under the influence of

[7]George Webb, *The Office and Authority of a Justice of Peace* (Williamsburg, 1736). William Simpson, *The Practical Justice of the Peace* (Charleston, 1761); *The County and Town Officer . . . of the Province of Massachusetts* (Boston, 1768); *An Abridgment of Burn's Justice of the Peace* (Boston, 1773); William Starke, *The Office and Authority of a Justice of the Peace* (Williamsburg, 1774); J. Davis, *The Office and Authority of a Justice of Peace* (New Bern, 1775); these titles are more fully described in James, "List," *Harvard Legal Essays,* 164, 167, 169, 175, 176, 177–78.

[8]John Adams's practice in Massachusetts is analyzed in Wroth and Zobel, eds., *Adams Legal Papers,* I, lx–lxi; the New York City practices of Benjamin Kissam and John Jay are described in Herbert A. Johnson, "John Jay: Colonial Lawyer" (Ph.D. diss., Columbia University, 1965), 30–31, 146–48.

[9]See Stanley N. Katz, "The Politics of Law in Colonial America: Controversies over Chancery Courts and Equity Law in the Eighteenth Century," *Perspectives in American History,* 5 (1971), 257–84; Joseph H.

seventeenth-century antipathy to equity jurisprudence, some colonies, like Massachusetts, eliminated chancery courts from their legal institutions, administering chancery business in the common law courts in a unique form of practice unknown in England or in the other American colonies to the south.[10] Other American jurisdictions, like Virginia, maintained a distinction between common law and chancery litigation, but left both types of cases to be administered in the same courts.[11] Although traditional distinctions remained, it is obvious that some modification and adaptation of the elaborate formalities of the English chancery court occurred in these circumstances. The third group of American jurisdictions, like New York and South Carolina, not only maintained separate chancery courts but also apparently followed most of the procedures developed in the English High Court of Chancery. Yet the colonial courts of chancery were cumbersome instruments of justice, presided over by governors often distracted by other affairs of state, and encumbranced by a full complement of clerks, solicitors, and counsellors. Attorneys' fees were high, and suits were attenuated in time and marked by prolixity of pleadings, resulting in a sparing recourse to chancery by colonial clients.[12] The peculiarities of colonial legal development coupled with the relative immaturity of the colonial social and economic fabric resulted in a lack of chancery business through-

---

Smith and Leo Hershkowitz, "Courts of Equity in the Province of New York: The Cosby Controversy, 1732–1736," *American Journal of Legal History,* 16 (1972), 1–50; Solon D. Wilson, "Courts of Chancery in the American Colonies," in Ernst Freund, ed., *Select Essays in Anglo-American Legal History,* 3 vols. (Boston, 1908), III, 779–809.

[10]Wroth and Zobel, *Adams Legal Papers,* I, xliii–xlv, 231–38.

[11]Oliver P. Chitwood, *Justice in Colonial Virginia* (Baltimore, 1905), 48; as to General Court see William Waller Hening, ed., *The Statutes at Large . . . of Virginia,* 13 vols. (New York, 1823), V, 467 at 470, 471, 484–88; as to the county courts see ibid., V, 489 at 491, 501–504.

[12]Johnson, "John Jay," *Univ. Pa. Law Rev.* 124, 1279–80.

out eighteenth-century America.[13] This situation is evidenced by the book purchases of the lawyers and judges of the time. It is also notable that among the Massachusetts practitioners included in this bibliography only Theophilus Parsons, who began practice late in the century, took the trouble to acquire a chancery manual; Parsons also had a post-Revolutionary practice that encompassed cases throughout the Middle Atlantic and New England states, bringing him into contact with other systems of equity jurisdiction.

Even rarer than chancery manuals in eighteenth-century American law libraries were manuals concerning admiralty practice. For the most part admiralty practice in the colonies was restricted to customs violations, breaches of the Navigation Acts, and prize cases, all which were outside the mainstream of work in the English High Court of Admiralty.[14] In addition cases appealed to England were retried by English proctors and advocates of the High Court, who upon occasion were known to comment upon the errors in the vice-admiralty procedure of the colonies.[15] Francis Clerke's admiralty manual was in the libraries of Thomas Jefferson and Theophilus Parsons, but John Adams, who had a most extensive vice-admiralty

[13]The removal of impediments to efficient court administration occurred after the American Revolution. Thereafter chancery business flourished in states which retained chancery courts or had created them after 1776.

[14]See Charles M. Hough, *Reports of Cases in the Vice Admiralty of the Province of New York and in the Court of Admiralty of the State of New York 1715–1788* (New Haven, 1925), and Dorothy S. Towle, ed., *Records of the Vice-Admiralty Court of Rhode Island* (Washington, D.C., 1936), for a general overview of the types of business handled by the colonial vice-admiralty courts.

[15]A detailed discussion of a New York vice-admiralty case is in Herbert A. Johnson and David Syrett, "Some Nice Sharp Quillets of the Customs Law: The *New York* Affair, 1763–1767," *William and Mary Quarterly,* 3rd ser., 25 (1968), 432–51. It was in this case that the English proctors complained about colonial procedures.

court practice before the Revolution, seems to have been able to survive without it or any similar guide to English admiralty procedure.

The small number of manuals in ecclesiastical court practice and the concentration of copies in the libraries of New York and southern lawyers suggest a regional interest in church court procedure. Because bishops of the Church of England had not been appointed for the American colonies, the probate jurisdiction normally exercised by their courts was delegated to the royal governors by action of the Crown. Each province developed its own procedures in matters of decedent estates, and the variations seem to have influenced lawyers in their acquisition of books on ecclesiastical law. New England and Pennsylvania followed a system of local probate in common law courts that substantially eliminated the need to refer to ecclesiastical-court form books. In New York a simplified form of English procedure was utilized, and there is some reason to believe that this was also the case in New Jersey, Maryland, Virginia, and South Carolina.[16] On the other hand, treatises on the substantive law of wills, intestate inheritance, and estate administration were widespread throughout the American colonies and states. Absent were detailed treatises on the canon law, regulations concerning the clergy, treatises on church court punishments for defamation, blasphemy, and related offenses, and similar works prepared and published in great numbers by the learned members of the Doctors' Commons of England. English ecclesiastical law had its greatest

[16]Wroth and Zobel, *Adams Legal Papers,* I, xliv, lv; Rush H. Limbaugh, "The Sources and Development of Probate Law," *1957 Washington University Law Quarterly,* 419, 427–35; Edith E. McQueen, "The Commissary in Colonial Maryland," *Maryland Historical Magazine,* 25 (1930), 190–206. On New York colonial procedure see Herbert A. Johnson, "The Prerogative Court of New York 1686–1776," *Am. Jour. of Legal History,* 17 (1973), 95, at 124–28, 141–42.

impact on the substantive aspects of American decedent estate practice, while the intricacies of church court procedures were for the most part ignored by American lawyers and judges.

A similar preference of substance over formalities seems to have been characteristic of American real property law in the eighteenth century. Although a number of real property treatises were imported from England and none was printed in the American colonies and states, the number of imported conveyancing manuals in this bibliography is much smaller than one would anticipate. American jurists of the eighteenth century did rely heavily upon English precedents, as can be seen from the widespread use of *The law of ejectments* and Sir Edward Coke's ever popular commentary upon Littleton's study of tenures. On the other hand, the detailed conveyancing formulas evolved by the English specialists in the field evidently were not essential for American practice. Quite possibly the listings may suggest that New England lawyers were not concerned with the English substantive law of real property, for their acquisitions in the field were negligible with the exception of the library of Theophilus Parsons. Certainly New England land law, based as much on seventeenth-century customs and usages in the Puritan colonies as upon English precedents, might be considered likely to diverge from that of the mother country.[17] But a less obvious but more widespread departure in the other colonies, accepting substan-

[17]Initial distribution of land in Massachusetts was made by allotments from the town trustees, and subsequent transfers were subject to recording in the town records. This system spread to the other New England settlements and Long Island, the latter development giving rise to the landmark case of Beers v. Hotchkiss, 256 N.Y. 41 (1931). See George L. Haskins, *Law and Authority in Early Massachusetts* (New York, 1960), 71–74, 171–73; George L. Haskins and Samuel E. Ewing, "The Spread of Massachusetts Law in the Seventeenth Century," in David H. Flaherty, ed., *Essays in the History of Early American Law* (Chapel Hill, N.C., 1969), 186–91.

tive rules but rejecting elaborate methods of conveyancing, has not been previously noted. The greater availability of land in America and its use as a commodity for speculation may explain the relative lack of interest in complete forms of conveyancing that would limit its alienability and preserve family landholdings intact. Whatever the underlying reasons may have been, it is apparent that in eighteenth-century America the bench and bar were primarily interested in the English substantive law of real property, and even within that framework New England jurists seem to have developed rules of real property law quite independent from those of England.

While Professor Joseph Smith's research[18] would indicate that New England jurisdictions, with the exception of Rhode Island, did not use the English substantive law of crime in any manner other than as a secondary or supplementary source of law, this bibliography suggests that acquisition of books on English criminal law was spread evenly throughout the American colonies and states.[19] Although the preparation of localized justice of the peace manuals for the American colonies and states would indicate some local variance from English procedures at the arraignment stage, the importation of Duncombe's *Tryals per pais* suggests reliance upon English criminal procedure at the trial level.[20]

A general interest in admiralty law and the law merchant is indicated by the acquisition of Molloy's *De jure maritimo* and Jacob's *Lex Mercatoria.* On the other hand these works were not widely supplemented by specialized treatises on negotiable instruments, bankruptcy, arbitration, and other fields within

[18]Joseph H. Smith, "The English Criminal Law in Early America," in *The English Legal System: Carryover to the Colonies* (Los Angeles, 1975), 3 at 22–29.

[19]On this see Julius Goebel, *Law Enforcement in Colonial New York, 1664–1776* (New York, 1944), *passim.*

[20]James, "List," *Harvard Legal Essays,* 184.

the law merchant. Also lacking is a representative group of the limited number of English treatises on prize law and the instance jurisdiction of admiralty courts. From this we may conclude perhaps that with the exception of an occasional collection action involving a negotiable instrument the average lawyer was not greatly concerned with commercial or admiralty litigation. The minutes of colonial vice-admiralty courts show the small number of instance cases tried in those courts and the small number of attorneys in regular practice at the admiralty bar.[21] Not surprisingly, the American bar in the early national period showed an amazing ignorance of prize procedure in England, which resulted in a sharp departure in American prize court practice from that in the mother country.[22]

Libraries of the colonial era evidenced an interest in the legal history of England that is far in excess of the normal requirements of law practice. Certainly eighteenth-century American practitioners knew more about English law of the medieval period than present-day lawyers know about the precedents of nineteenth-century America. They also were conversant, as their libraries show, with the extant sources for study of Roman law and with commentaries or summaries of Scottish and continental legal history. By current-day academic standards the eighteenth-century lawyer's understanding of these subjects may be considered deficient, but his breadth of concern for historical study surely exceeds that of the practitioner of the twentieth century. To a considerable degree an interest in the history of law and an inquiring mind concerning the law of other nations and cultures were products of the liberal education afforded the young man who as-

[21]See the printed records cited at n. 14 above; there are also microfilm records for the South Carolina vice-admiralty court. Microfilm T-299, National Archives, Washington, D.C.

[22]Henry J. Bourguignon, *The First Federal Court, 1775–1787* (Philadelphia, 1977), 181–87.

pired to the legal profession after completing his collegiate education. More than in our age, the eighteenth century sought universals in human experience, and it might be anticipated that men of the law would seek common denominators by comparison of Anglo-American law with that of foreign nations. Natural law was also a subject introduced into a would-be lawyer's education at the collegiate level, and for that reason it is not surprising to find libraries containing one or more of the works of Baron von Pufendorf.[23] Lawyers in an age of reason sought in the immutable principles of the law of nature the foundation for man-made laws and regulations, as well as a legitimization of national and municipal law through its conformity with the historical practices of mankind.

The daily demands of practice seem to have a strong influence on the book acquisitions of American lawyers and judges in the eighteenth century. This bibliography indicates their preferences for general treatises and for subjects which were central to American law and procedure. On the other hand, as learned men they also recognized an obligation to remain familiar with those writings in the fields of legal history, natural law, and foreign law which would provide a balanced and cosmopolitan view of jurisprudence. Indeed it is important that twentieth-century readers appreciate the fact that educated men of the eighteenth century would not have accepted our narrow view of the scope of legal education and study. Law was part and parcel of the knowledge of an informed citizen, regardless of his profession; conversely, the lawyer who would presume to success in his profession read far beyond the limits

[23]Grotius, *The Law of War and Peace,* and Baron von Pufendorf's *Law of Nations* were in the fourth-year curriculum at King's College. *Columbia University, Early Minutes of the Trustees, Vol. I, 1755–1770* (New York, 1932), Mar. 1, 1763. Jasper Yeates's copies of these titles bear inscriptions indicating that he used the books while a student at the College of Philadelphia.

of "black letter law." A vigorous study of the classics of Greek and Roman antiquity, a knowledge of the growing fields of moral and natural philosophy, and a ready acquaintance with English literature were integral parts of the education of an eighteenth-century lawyer. All were reflected in his library holdings, and undoubtedly influenced the scholarly aspects of his practice.

Economics would dictate that book purchases for such scholarly reasons be postponed until the more practical needs of everyday use could be satisfied. Yet on the balance the law library of the average American lawyer of the eighteenth century reveals him as a competent professional with interests in the law that transcended the demands of office business and litigation. Certain of these lawyers, such as Thomas Jefferson and John Adams, achieved such positions that their book acquisitions ranged over the entire field of law and into subjects we would classify today as political theory and the social sciences. Quite possibly some of the other practitioners whose libraries are summarized in this bibliography would have assembled similar collections if their means and opportunities had permitted them to do so. This is evident by the quality of books they did own.

This taste for English legal treatises was clearly not limited to men who had received their formal legal education at the English Inns of Court. Indeed the customs of the various colonies differed in the attitude of colonial lawyers toward training at the Inns. In New York it was considered not only a useless and expensive appendage to clerkship but also a dangerous threat to the morals of the young clerk.[24] Conversely, colonial South Carolina required attendance at the Inns as a prerequisite of admission to the bar; this tradition continued well into the national period even though not so required by

[24]Hamlin, *Legal Education,* 12–20.

court rules.[25] Yet the libraries of men from these two colonies reflect interests developed not from early training but from practical needs recognized by practitioners in colonial courts.

Bibliographies serve a variety of purposes. They can be used for the narrow function of identifying and locating published books on a given subject, and they can also be used for the broader knowledge that they provide concerning the intellectual history of an individual or group.[26] Like other bibliographies, this modest effort perhaps will serve both functions. Nevertheless, this work will have met the author's purpose well if it provides legal historians some general idea of the importance of a given treatise to early American law.

[25]Gregorie, ed., *Chancery Minutes of South Carolina,* 15; Donald J. Senese, "Legal Thought in South Carolina" (Ph.D. diss., Univ. of South Carolina, 1970), 29.

[26]A good use of law library holdings for intellectual history purposes is Edwin Wolf 2nd, "Historical Development of the American Lawyer's Library [Eighteenth Century]," *Law Library Journal,* 61 (1959), 440–50. See also Louis B. Wright, *The First Gentlemen of Virginia* (Charlottesville, 1964), 117–54.

ACKNOWLEDGMENTS

A legal historian venturing into the field of bibliography encumbers himself with numerous debts of gratitude that can only be discharged in part by an acknowledgment to his creditors. When the idea of a bibliography of imported law treatises was brought to the attention of the University of Tennessee Press, the staff was most encouraging and urged its compilation not only as a guide to book acquisitions by early American lawyers, but also as an initial step that might at some future date make those titles available for scholarly use in the form of a microcard or microfiche edition. Without that early expression of interest the task would never have been undertaken. Without a group of helpful and encouraging librarians and bibliographers it would not have been possible to complete it. John D. Cushing of the Massachusetts Historical Society; Walter B. Edgar of the University of South Carolina history department; Etta Falkner of the Old Sturbridge Village research department; Mary M.R. Goodwin of the Colonial Williamsburg research department; Henry D. Grunder, curator of rare books at the Swem Library of the College of William and Mary; Edith G.Henderson of the Harvard Law Library; James Madison Whitehead, formerly law librarian at the College of William and Mary; Raymond V. Shepherd, administrator of Cliveden; John V. Aungst, administrator of the Lancaster County Historical Society; James Lawton, curator of rare books at the Boston Public Library; and Edwin Wolf 2nd, librarian of the Library Company of Philadelphia, have been unselfish in sharing with me their knowledge of early American law libraries. In its final stages the manuscript benefitted from a critical reading by George M. Curtis III, research associate on *The Papers of John Marshall* staff.

Work on the text of this bibliography was greatly accelerated by my appointment as Lucy Hampton Bostick visiting research professor at the Southern Studies Program of the University of South Carolina. I had the enviable opportunity to continue my work in company with James B. Meriwether, director of the Southern Studies Program and an outstanding bibliographer, and Noel Polk, bibliographer at the Southern Studies Program. Linda McDonald, a graduate student at the Southern Studies Program and presently a law student at the University of South Carolina Law School, undertook the onerous task of bibliographical verification of the entries with a spirit of enthusiasm and diligence that was exceeded only by her care and competence. She has greatly increased the accuracy of the entries and made an outstanding contribution to the progress of this endeavor. Finally, my wife, Barbara, patiently endured nocturnal typing while my days were occupied with full-time editorial work on *The Papers of John Marshall.* She also contributed in a number of other ways to provide time and opportunity for me to continue this project and to encourage its completion.

WILLIAMSBURG
AUGUST 1977

Herbert A. Johnson

METHOD, APPARATUS, AND ABBREVIATIONS

This is a composite bibliography developed through the examination of extant eighteenth-century law libraries and the reconstruction of other libraries from surviving lists or estate inventories showing library holdings. While a number of law books of the eighteenth century are available for use in libraries throughout the United States, there are very few eighteenth-century law libraries maintained in their original state. Until recently librarians have been remiss in recording the provenance of their acquisitions, and this has resulted in the merger of a number of private libraries into the larger undifferentiated collections of their current owners. With progression of the *National Union Catalog* toward completion these individual titles can be located with ease by legal historians seeking access to any particular book. Yet the acquisition of books by lawyers of the eighteenth century cannot be studied satisfactorily through the location of individual titles once owned by them.

Because this bibliography attempts to assemble in a convenient form a list of imported law books that were in active use in eighteenth-century America, we have made no effort to locate individual extant copies of a title. The books listed, however, are all part of identifiable collections of law books, either extant or represented by lists, which once belonged to an American lawyer or judge. Although this listing may provide a useful guide to the location of copies of a given title, the wise research scholar will verify the location of other copies in the *National Union Catalog* before undertaking an expensive journey to a distant rare book library.

The rich collection in Thomas Jefferson's library, retrieved from bibliographical obscurity by the painstaking work of E. Millicent Sowerby,[1] is a national treasure that makes the Library of Congress of major interest to legal historians. Although law books constitute no more than a quarter of the Jefferson collection, they nevertheless constitute the largest complete law library dating from the eighteenth century in the United States. Next in size and importance is the slightly more modest collection of John Adams, maintained at the Boston Public Library.[2] Again the Adams library is far more extensive than its legal holdings, demonstrating the breadth of mind that was characteristic of the second President of the United States. These large and well-known collections are supplemented by two extensive, yet little used, libraries. The library of Chief Justice Benjamin Chew of Pennsylvania is a remarkably complete collection of eighteenth-century law books, preserved until recently by the Chew family and now housed at Cliveden under the administration of the National Trust for Historic Preservation. Currently being cataloged by the staff at Cliveden, the family collection may soon be open for scholarly use. Another Pennsylvania library of substantial size and quality is that of Justice Jasper Yeates, owned by the Lancaster County Bar Association and administered by the Lancaster County Historical Society. Although the Yeates library is particularly rich in holdings, it has not been arranged for scholarly use, and while the staff at the historical society is

[1]E. Millicent Sowerby, ed., *Catalogue of the Library of Thomas Jefferson*, 5 vols. (Washington, D.C., 1952).

[2]See Lindsay Swift, ed., *Catalogue of the John Adams Library in the Public Library of the city of Boston* (Boston, 1917).

eager to make it available, there is considerable difficulty in finding titles on the shelves. Properly arranged and cataloged, the Yeates library would rival those of Adams, Jefferson, and Chew in its value for legal historians.

Smaller in size than these libraries but substantially complete in its eighteenth-century form is the collection of St. George Tucker, the Virginia jurist and American editor of Blackstone's *Commentaries.* Maintained by generations of the Tucker family and recently donated by them to the College of William and Mary, the Tucker library is particularly rich in late eighteenth-century and early nineteenth-century legal pamphlets and other fugitive materials. On the other hand it is representative of the reading habits and professional research requirements of a practitioner at the end of the eighteenth century. The libraries of John Jay, first chief justice of the United States, and attorney Joseph Murray of New York survive in the Treasure Room of the Columbia Law Library. While both are good representative collections, they were probably much larger in the lifetimes of their original owners than they are at the present time.[3] Neither of these New York libraries demonstrates the scope of intellectual activity characteristic of the Adams and Jefferson collections, and while neither may be useful as a guide to the reading habits of its owner, each does indicate the professional sources the owner considered most essential to his law practice.

[3]John Jay's remaining books show signs of damage, probably attributable to the American evacuation of New York City in 1776, and his papers contain some evidence of the problem of moving his law office library from the city. Johnson, "John Jay: Colonial Lawyer," 174–75. Murray's books, donated to King's College before the Revolution, may have been decimated by neglect and theft during the suspension of college activities from 1776 until the British surrendered New York City in 1784. See Horace Coon, *Columbia: Colossus on the Hudson* (New York, 1947), 55; David C. Humphrey, *From King's College to Columbia, 1746–1800* (New York, 1976), 130, 153, 276, 287, 290.

The abundance of titles in the libraries of Adams and Jefferson could easily create difficulties in a bibliography such as this, which seeks to measure the influence of authors and books over a broad spectrum of eighteenth-century jurists. Both Presidents served in diplomatic posts that permitted them wider access to British and European book markets than lawyers who had remained at home. In addition each may be said to have exhibited certain tendencies of the bibliophile, an avocation not financially or geographically feasible for most practitioners and judges in the colonies and states. Quite clearly both the Adams and Jefferson libraries contain titles that are held by no other lawyer or judge in the group of libraries assembled here; moreover, if other libraries did hold only one copy of an otherwise unknown title, that in itself does not indicate any substantial utilization of the book. Consequently for the purposes of this bibliography the rule that at least two copies of any title must be identifiable in at least two eighteenth-century libraries before the title will be included herein. The inclusion of single titles from either the Adams or the Jefferson libraries would have certainly doubled, if not tripled, the length of this bibliography, thereby detracting from its usefulness and adding no information that is not already available from the printed bibliographies of those libraries.

To supplement information available from existing libraries, library lists prepared by the owner or by the executors or administrators of his estate have been used. As Edwin Wolf 2nd has commented, such lists are *rarissimae avis,*[4] and it would be presumptuous to claim that all such lists have been included in this bibliography. On the other hand an effort has been made to obtain a sampling of such lists for each colony and for

[4]In "The Library of Ralph Assheton: The Book Background of a Colonial Philadelphia Lawyer," *Papers of the Bibliographical Society of America,* 58 (1964), 345.

a variety of time periods throughout the eighteenth century. Despite their rarity the lists are more common than extant law libraries, and they form the major portion of the source material for this bibliography. Paul M. Hamlin included a fine set of law library lists in his 1939 doctoral dissertation on legal education.[5] A representative group of libraries from those lists is included, certain ones having been excluded as not representing lawyers' and judges' libraries and others because their inclusion would either duplicate copies in the hands of subsequent owners or imbalance the sample of libraries in favor of New York collections. For example, Hamlin lists the library of Judge John Chambers, which survives in part in the extant library of his nephew and godson, John Jay. Similarly the library of Governor John Montgomerie, auctioned early in the century, can be found in a number of the other law libraries assembled by later generations of New Yorkers active in the law. Both have been excluded.

The printed library lists of William Byrd II and Robert "King" Carter have been scanned for legal titles, and these have been included, along with the more scholarly library lists prepared and annotated for Ralph Assheton and John Guest by Edwin Wolf 2nd. Manuscript lists have been utilized to reconstruct the holdings of the libraries of Francis Dana, James Grindlay, Peter Leigh, John Mercer, Benet Oldham, and Robert T. Paine, and a master's essay comprising a bibliography of St. George Tucker's library has been helpful in retrieving titles not currently in that collection. The collection of Theophilus Parsons was reconstructed from an auction catalog issued in 1814 in connection with the sale of his books.[6]

Library lists and auction catalogs are far from the most

[5]Hamlin, *Legal Education,* appendix 7, 171–96.

[6]Full citations are given after the names of the owners in the List of Libraries and Owners.

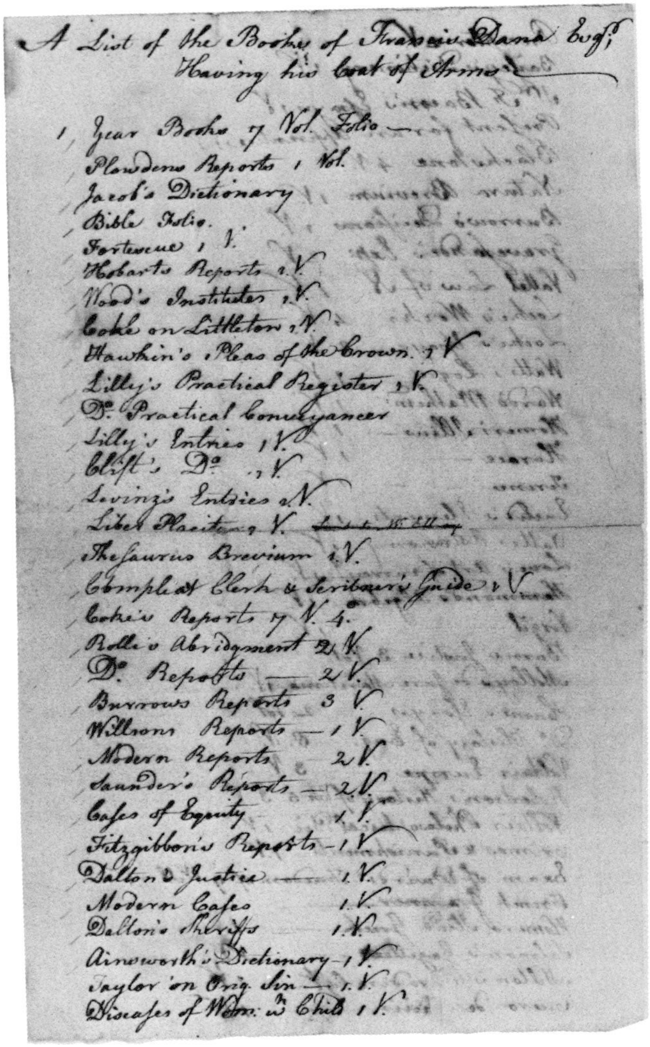

A List of the Books of Francis Dana Esq;
Having his Coat of Arms

1, Year Books 7 Vol. Folio —
Plowdens Reports 1 Vol.
Jacob's Dictionary
Bible Folio.
Fortescue 1 V.
Hobarts Reports 1 V.
Wood's Institutes 1 V.
Coke on Littleton 1 V.
Hawkin's Pleas of the Crown. 1 V.
Lilly's Practical Register 1 V.
D°. Practical Conveyancer
Lilly's Entries 1 V.
Clift's D°. 1 V.
Levinz's Entries 1 V.
Liber Placitandi 1 V.
Thesaurus Brevium 1 V.
Compleat Clerk & Scrivener's Guide 1 V.
Coke's Reports 7 V. 4°.
Rolle's Abridgment 2 V.
D°. Reports — 2 V.
Burrows Reports 3 V.
Willsons Reports — 1 V.
Modern Reports 2 V.
Saunder's Reports — 2 V.
Cases of Equity 1 V.
Fitzgibbon's Reports — 1 V.
Dalton's Justice — 1 V.
Modern Cases 1 V.
Dalton's Sheriffs 1 V.
Ainsworth's Dictionary — 1 V.
Taylor on Orig. Sin — 1 V.
Diseases of Wom. & Child 1 V.

The Library List of Francis Dana.
Francis Dana Papers, Massachusetts Historical Society, Boston.

satisfactory sources of bibliographical information. Titles are incomplete and books are occasionally cited by author, title, or both. In most cases edition identification is not possible, even when the volume size is provided. There is also some confusion when one or more imprints are identified by the same short title. With this thicket of entangling evidence it has seemed wise to ignore those entries on lists and in the catalog which are ambiguous.

Extensive advertisements offering a large number of books for sale appeared in colonial newspapers published in the major cities of eighteenth-century America. The variety of titles is remarkable when one compares the rich selection of books available with the fairly constant preference of lawyers and judges for a restricted number of titles. Clearly the booksellers in colonial America were much more optimistic about the market for law books than this bibliography would indicate they should have been. On the other hand it is quite possible that only a few copies of each title were imported as a means of increasing interest in newly published books, and continued efforts to sell those volumes through newspaper advertisements may well provide the historian with an erroneous impression that the booksellers were not in touch with the purchasing tastes of their clients. These considerations are adequate in themselves to cast doubt upon the wisdom of using booksellers' advertisements as a source for judging the colonial book trade. In addition there is the unquestioned fact that Americans bought their books not only from local booksellers, but also directly from English booksellers and publishers. For these reasons we have ignored booksellers' advertisements as a mode of gauging the impact of imported law treatises upon the American bench and bar.

The term "law treatises" may be broadly or narrowly construed, and it is helpful to identify the criteria established for this bibliography. The standard fields of English law, in its public and private spheres, have been included, as have those of Scottish and Irish law. Also included are treatises on Roman law, continental and foreign law, international law, and natural law. Excluded have been works on political science or theory, philosophical tracts (except jurisprudence), and historical works not identifiable as legal history. Much of the work in fields currently termed the social sciences can be connected with legal studies, but except where these studies are directly pertinent to the work of the courts, they have been excluded in this compilation. The growing interest in political theory, witnessed by a number of holdings of Montesquieu, Burlamaqui, and Locke, and the concern for penology, evidenced by holdings of Beccaria, are therefore not reflected in this bibliography.

As noted previously this compilation does not contain imprints of the statutes, either enactments of Parliament or those of sister colonies. Nor does it contain the standard English case reports available in *English Reports, Full Reprint.* It does include, however, abridgments of the statutes and abridgments of cases, as well as pamphlet publications of significant cases that may or may not have been included in subsequent law reports. These rules have been followed concerning foreign materials, except that in regard to Roman law it has been decided to include citations to the *Corpus Juris Civilis* and the *Digest* and *Institutes* of Justinian as if they were treatises rather than an accumulation of case law and statutory materials.

English titles have been initially checked against the Sweet and Maxwell bibliography of law books, and then they and other titles in Scottish or foreign law have been cross-checked to the *National Union Catalog,* the *Library of Congress Catalog,* and the *British Museum Catalog.* We have preferred the punctuation and capitalization of the first imprint of any given title issued in the eighteenth century and have indicated by footnotes any variations in subsequent editions. When a seventeenth-century title has been used in the eighteenth century as a convenient mode of identification for later editions of the book, that use is also noted.

Editions of a work are identified by the number of the edition and by any indication of the manner in which its contents were changed from previous editions. When, in some instances, the number of a particular edition cannot be provided, the date and place of publication are given instead. While an attempt has been made to supply the publisher's name for each title and each edition of a title, at times these details are not available; in these cases the missing information has been indicated by a blank space. Naturally when no information is available to identify the holding of a given library other than by author and title, no edition, date, or place of publication has been supplied.

Holdings of individual libraries are shown by the original owner's name. If the title is unidentifiable as to its edition, the owner's name is placed immediately after the title of the work. On the other hand, if the edition in the library is known, the owner's name will appear immediately after the bibliographic reference to that particular edition. Where a library contained only part of a multi-volume set, that fact is reflected in a footnote. The listings also distinguish between extant and reconstructed libraries; extant libraries are listed by the owner's name, followed by the *National Union Catalog* symbol for the present location of the library. Reconstructed libraries are identified by the owner's name, followed by an asterisk (*), with a parenthetical reference to the page of the printed or manuscript list upon which the title appears. Naturally where a manuscript library list is unpaginated, such as occurs in the cases of Benjamin Chew, Francis Dana, and Robert Treat Paine, no parenthetical notation follows the asterisk.

The title used is that of the first edition published in the eighteenth century. When the title varies in subsequent editions, a footnote provides the variation. The few titles published in the American colonies or states during the eighteenth century are listed in Eldon R. James, "A List of Treatises Printed in the British Colonies and the American States before 1801," *Harvard Legal Essays* (Cambridge, Mass., 1934), 159–211. Footnotes to those titles refer the reader to numbers in the James bibliography which relate to those works.

The index for the present bibliography has been prepared to provide a cross reference between authors' names and titles, which may prove valuable for the reader to find the many treatises that are cited either by author or by title in eighteenth-century citations. In addition the appendix, listing entries in terms of frequency of use and category, will be helpful in identifying books that were imported in the eighteenth century.

National Union Catalog symbols and similar symbols devised for use in this bibliography are as follows:

DLC	The Library of Congress, Washington, D.C.
MB	Boston Public Library, Boston
MStOSV	McClellan Law Office, Old Sturbridge Village, Sturbridge, Massachusetts
NNC-L	Columbia University Law Library, New York
PLHi	Lancaster County Historical Society, Lancaster, Pennsylvania
PPCl	Cliveden, Philadelphia
PPL	Library Company of Philadelphia, Philadelphia
ViW	College of William and Mary Library, Williamsburg, Virginia

LIST OF LIBRARIES AND OWNERS

John Adams (1735–1826), second President of the United States. Attended Harvard College (A.B. 1755; M.A. 1758). Studied law under James Putnam. Admitted to practice in Massachusetts in 1768 and continued in practice until the American Revolution. His library is maintained at the Boston Public Library (MB) and is described in Lindsay Swift, ed., *Catalogue of the John Adams Library in the Public Library of the city of Boston* (Boston, 1917).

James Alexander (1691–1756), attorney and surveyor. Studied law by clerkship in New York. Admitted to practice in New Jersey in 1723. Served as co-counsel for John Peter Zenger in 1735 and as attorney general of New Jersey 1723–27. A founder of the American Philosophical Society. His library holdings are based upon a March 20, 1720 list, reprinted in Paul M. Hamlin, *Legal Education in Colonial New York* (New York, 1939), 171–76.

Ralph Assheton (1695–1746), lawyer and judge. Clerked with his father, Robert Assheton, and admitted to practice in 1720. Town clerk of Philadelphia, 1716–46. Judge of the Pennsylvania Court of Chancery, 1730–35; judge of the Court of Common Pleas, 1738–46. His library holdings are based upon his estate inventory of books, published in Edwin Wolf 2nd, "The Library of Ralph Assheton: The Book

Background of a Colonial Philadelphia Lawyer," *The Papers of the Bibliographical Society of America,* 51 (1964), 345–79.

William Byrd II (1674–1744), planter, barrister, and colonial official. Studied at the Middle Temple in 1692. Virginia agent in London, 1698–1704 and 1710–20. Receiver general of Virginia, 1706–10. Member of the Council of State, 1709–44. His library holdings are based upon a 1777 list of Byrd's library, which was sold in the same year; the list is published in John Spencer Bassett, *The Writings of "Colonel William Byrd of Westover in Virginia Esqr."* (New York, 1901), 413–43.

Robert Carter ["King" Carter] (1663–1732), planter and colonial official. Member of the Council of State, 1699–1732. Treasurer of Virginia, 1699–1705. Agent for Lord Fairfax, proprietor of the Northern Neck, 1702–11 and 1722–32. His library holdings are based upon his estate inventory of books and other personalty, published in "Carter Papers," *Virginia Historical Magazine,* 6 (1898–99), 145–52, 260–70.

Benjamin Chew (1722–1810), attorney and judge. Read law with Andrew Hamilton c 1740–41. Admitted to Middle Temple, 1743. Admitted to practice in Pennsylvania, 1746; practiced in Delaware in 1746–54 and in Pennsylvania, 1754–74. Attorney general of Pennsylvania, 1755–69. Recorder of Philadelphia, 1774–76. Member of the Provincial Council, 1755–76. Chief justice of the Supreme Court of Pennsylvania, 1774–76. Judge and president of the Pennsylvania High Court of Errors and Appeals, 1791–1810. His library is at Cliveden, Philadelphia; non-extant volumes are listed from a library list in the manuscript collection at Cliveden.

Francis Dana (1743–1811), attorney, diplomat, and judge. Attended Harvard College (A.B. 1762; M.A. 1765).

Clerked with Edmund Trowbridge. Admitted to practice in Massachusetts in 1767, and continued in practice until the American Revolution. Minister to Russia, 1781–83. Chief justice of the Supreme Judicial Court of Massachusetts, 1791–1806. His library holdings are based upon a manuscript list in the Francis Dana Papers, Massachusetts Historical Society, Boston.

James Grindlay (d 1765), attorney. A native of Scotland, he was in practice before the South Carolina Court of Common Pleas c 1745–65. His library holdings are based upon a manuscript estate inventory recorded in Inventories, 1763–67, pp. 280–84, South Carolina Department of Archives and History, Columbia.

John Guest (c 1650–1707), judge and public official. Attended Pembroke College, Oxford, 1670 and Pembroke College, Cambridge (A.B. 1672). Entered studies at Lincoln's Inn, 1670. Chief justice of the Supreme Court of Pennsylvania, 1701–1706. Presiding justice of the Philadelphia Court of Quarter Sessions, 1703–1704. Member of the Provincial Council, 1701–1707. His library holdings are based upon an estate inventory of July 19, 1708, printed in Edwin Wolf 2nd, "The Library of a Philadelphia Judge, 1708," *Pennsylvania Magazine of History and Biography,* 83 (1959), 180–91.

John Jay (1745–1829), first chief justice of the United States. Attended King's College, now Columbia University (A.B. 1764; M.A. 1767). Studied law under Benjamin Kissam. Admitted to practice in New York in 1768. Chief justice of the Supreme Court of New York, 1777–78. Chief justice of the United States, 1789–95. His library holdings are based upon a physical examination of his books in the Treasure Room, Columbia University Law Library (NNC-L), reported in Herbert A.

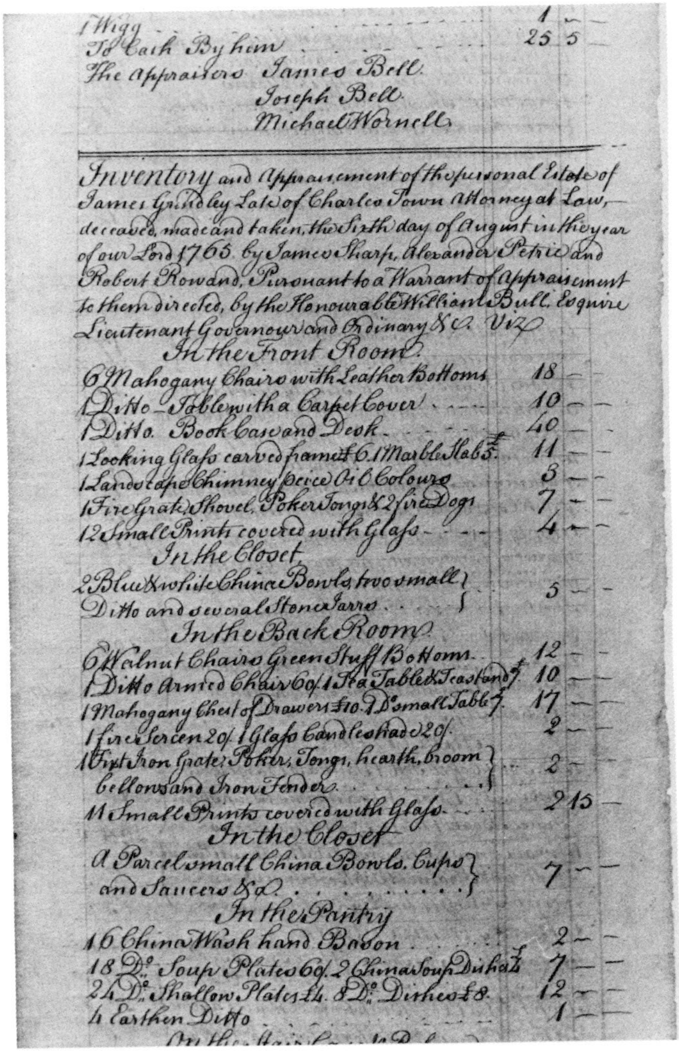

1 Wigg	1	—	—
To Cash By him	25	5	—

The appraisers James Bell
Joseph Bell
Michael Wornell

Inventory and Appraisement of the personal Estate of James Grindley Late of Charles Town Attorney at Law, deceased, made and taken the Sixth day of August in the year of our Lord 1765 by James Sharp, Alexander Petrie and Robert Rowand, Pursuant to a Warrant of Appraisement to them directed, by the Honourable William Bull Esquire Lieutenant Governour and Ordinary &c. Viz

In the Front Room

	£	s	d
6 Mahogany Chairs with Leather Bottoms	18	—	—
1 Ditto Table with a Carpet Cover	10	—	—
1 Ditto Book Case and Desk	40	—	—
1 Looking Glass carved frame £6. 1 Marble Slab £5	11	—	—
1 Landscape Chimney peice Oil Colours	3	—	—
1 Fire Grate Shovel, Poker Tongs & 2 fire Dogs	7	—	—
12 Small Prints covered with Glass	4	—	—

In the Closet

2 Blue & white China Bowls two small Ditto and several Stone Jarrs	5	—	—

In the Back Room

6 Walnut Chairs Green Stuff Bottoms	12	—	—
1 Ditto Armed Chair 60/ 1 Tea Table & Teastand £7	10	—	—
1 Mahogany Chest of Drawers £10. 1 D° small Table £7	17	—	—
1 fire Screen 20/ 1 Glass Candleshade 20/	2	—	—
1 Fixt Iron Grate, Poker, Tongs, hearth broom bellows and Iron Fender	2	—	—
11 Small Prints covered with Glass	2	15	—

In the Closet

A Parcel small China Bowls, Cups and Saucers &c	7	—	—

In the Pantry

16 China Wash hand Bason	2	—	—
18 D° Soup Plates 60/ 2 China Soup Dishes £4	7	—	—
24 D° Shallow Plates £4. 8 D° Dishes £8	12	—	—
4 Earthen Ditto	1	—	—

In the Stair Case ...

Estate Inventory of James Grindlay.
South Carolina Department of Archives and History, Columbia.

Johnson, "John Jay: Colonial Lawyer" (Ph.D. diss., Columbia Univ., 1965), 264–72.

Thomas Jefferson, third President of the United States. Attended the College of William and Mary (A.B. 1762). Studied law under George Wythe. Admitted to practice in Virginia in 1767 and continued in practice until the American Revolution. His law library is at the Library of Congress (DLC), and non-extant holdings are cited in E. Millicent Sowerby, ed., *Catalogue of the Library of Thomas Jefferson,* II (Washington, D.C., 1953).

Peter Leigh (d 1759), judge. High bailiff of Westminster, 1739. Chief justice of South Carolina, 1753–59. His library holdings are based upon a manuscript estate inventory recorded in Inventories, T, 256–57, South Carolina Department of Archives and History, Columbia.

James Logan (1671–1751), scholar and judge. Privately tutored in Greek, Latin, and Hebrew. Member of the Provincial Council of Pennsylvania, 1702–47. Judge of the Philadelphia Court of Common Pleas, 1727–31. Chief justice of the Supreme Court of Pennsylvania, 1731–39. His library is at the Library Company of Philadelphia (PPL) and non-extant holdings are based upon Edwin Wolf 2nd, *The Library of James Logan of Philadelphia 1674–1751* (Philadelphia, 1974).

John McClellan (1767–1858), attorney. Attended Yale College (A.B. 1785). Studied law under Samuel Huntington. Admitted to practice in Connecticut, 1787. Justice of the peace for Woodstock. His library is located at the law office, Old Sturbridge Village, Sturbridge, Massachusetts.

John Mercer (1704–68), attorney. Attended Trinity College, Dublin. In practice in Virginia c 1728. Compiler in 1737 and 1759 of an abridgment of Virginia statutes. Secretary of the Ohio Company. His library holdings are based on an inventory transcribed in an account book maintained at the Bucks County Historical Society, Doylestown, Pennsylvania.

Joseph Murray (c 1694–1757), attorney. Admitted to practice in New York City Mayor's Court, 1718. Admitted to the Inner Temple, 1725. Admitted to practice in New York in 1728. Member of the Provincial Council, 1743–53. Member of the first board of trustees and governor of the New York Society Library. Governor of King's College, 1754–57. His library, donated to King's College, is maintained at the Columbia University Law Library.

Benet Oldham (d 1768). A South Carolina lawyer who had been admitted to practice before the South Carolina Court of Chancery in 1764. His library holdings are based upon a manuscript estate inventory recorded in Inventories, X, 407–408, South Carolina Department of Archives and History, Columbia.

Robert Treat Paine (1731–1814), lawyer and judge. Attended Harvard College (A.B. 1749). Clerked with Benjamin Pratt. Admitted to Massachusetts bar in 1757 and practiced in Portland, Maine, and Taunton, Massachusetts. Associate prosecuting attorney at Boston Massacre trial, 1770. Attorney general of Massachusetts, 1777–90. Associate justice of the Supreme Judicial Court of Massachusetts, 1790–1804. Founder of the American Academy of Arts and Sciences, 1780. His library is reconstructed from two manuscript catalogs contained in the Robert Treat Paine Papers, Massachusetts Historical Society.

Theophilus Parsons (1750–1813), judge. Attended Harvard College (A.B. 1769). Studied law under Theophilus Bradbury. Admitted to practice in Massachusetts in 1774 and continued in practice during and after the American Revolution. Chief justice of the Supreme Judicial Court of Massachusetts, 1806–13. Principal founder of the Boston Athenaeum and a founder of the Social Law Library. Fellow of Harvard College, 1806–13. His library holdings are based upon *Catalogue of the Library of the Hon. Theophilus Parsons. To be sold by auction March 1st. 1814, at the store of Francis Amory, No. 41, Marlboro' Street* (Boston, 1814), 17–23.

William Smith, Sr. (1697–1769), judge. Attended Yale College (A.B. 1719; M.A. 1722); tutor at Yale College, 1722–24. Admitted to practice law in New York, 1724. Admitted to Gray's Inn, 1727. Co-counsel for John Peter Zenger, 1735. Attorney general of New York, 1751–52. Member of the Provincial Council, 1753–67. Associate justice of the Supreme Court of Judicature, 1763–67. A founder of the first public school in New York City, 1732. An incorporator of the College of New Jersey (now Princeton University), 1746. A founder and trustee of the New York Society Library. His library holdings are based upon a 1770 estate inventory printed in Hamlin, *Legal Education,* 182–92.

St. George Tucker (1752–1827), editor of Blackstone's *Commentaries* and judge. Attended the College of William and Mary (A.B. 1772). Studied law under George Wythe. Admitted to practice in Virginia in 1775 and resumed practice after the American Revolution. Judge of the General Court, 1788–1803. Professor of Law and Police, College of William and Mary, 1800–11. Judge of the Court of Appeals of Virginia, 1803–11. United States District Judge, 1811–27. Annotator of Blackstone's *Commentaries* (5 vols., 1803). His library is at the Swem Library, College of William and Mary, and non-extant holdings are based upon Jill M. Coghlan, "The Library of St. George Tucker" (M.A. thesis, College of William and Mary, 1973).

Jasper Yeates (1745–1817), lawyer and judge. Attended College of Philadelphia (A.B. 1761). Clerked with Edward Shippen. Admitted to practice in Pennsylvania in 1765 and established his practice in Lancaster. Associate justice of the Supreme Court of Pennsylvania, 1791–1817. Reporter of opinions of the Supreme Court of Pennsylvania, 1791–1808. His library is at the Lancaster County Historical Society, Lancaster.

IMPORTED EIGHTEENTH-CENTURY LAW TREATISES IN AMERICAN LIBRARIES 1700–1799

BIBLIOGRAPHY

1 Adams, John. *A Defense of the Constitutions of Government of the United States of America.*
Robert Treat Paine.*

3 vols., London: C. Dilly, 1787. John Adams, MB.[1]

2 Bacon, Sir Francis. *Law Tracts.*

1st ed., London: E. and R. Nutt, 1737. Benjamin Chew, PPCl.

2nd ed., London: Dan. Browne, 1741. Jasper Yeates, PLHi.

3 Bacon, Matthew. *The Compleat Arbitrator; or, The Law of Awards . . . .*

3rd ed., London: J. Worrall and R. Tovey, 1770. William Smith, Sr.* (188); Theophilus Parsons* (19).

4 Bacon, Matthew. *A New Abridgment of the Law.*
James Grindlay* (281); St. George Tucker* (70).

5 vols., London: E. and R. Nutt, 1736–66. John Adams, MB; Benjamin Chew, PPCl; Peter Leigh*[2] (256); Jasper Yeates, PLHi.[3]

[1]The Adams library also contains the two-volume French edition, published by Buisson in Paris in 1792.

[2]Vols. 1, 2, and 3 only.

[3]Vol. 5 only.

3rd ed., corrected and enlarged, 5 vols., London: J. Worrall & Co., A. Shuckburgh, T. Waller, 1768. Jasper Yeates, PLHi.[4]

4th ed., 5 vols., London: W. Strahan & M. Woodfall, 1778. Theophilus Parsons* (18).

5th ed., 5 vols., Dublin: J. Exshaw, 1786. John McClellan, MStOSV.

5th ed., 5 vols., London: T. Cadell, C. Dilly, G.G. and J. Robinson, 1798. Thomas Jefferson, DLC.

5 Ballow, Henry. *A Treatise of Equity . . . .*
Robert Treat Paine.*

1st ed., London: D. Browne and J. Shuckburgh, 1737. Thomas Jefferson, DLC; John Mercer* (200).

3rd ed., enlarged, John Fonblanque, ed., 2 vols., Dublin: P. Byrne, J. Moore, W. Jones, 1793–95. Jasper Yeates, PLHi.

6 Barnes, Henry. *Notes of Cases in Points of Practice: taken in the Court of Common Pleas at Westminster . . . 1732, to . . . 1754.*

2 vols., London: Henry Lintot, 1754. Benjamin PPCl; James Grindlay* (282); William Smith, Sr.* (192); Jasper Yeates, PLHi.

7 *Baron and Feme. A Treatise of the Common Law Concerning Husbands and Wives . . . .*[5]
William Byrd II* (418); John Mercer* (200).

[4]Vols. 1–4 only.

[5]The subtitle to the third edition is *A Treatise of Law and Equity, Concerning Husbands and Wives . . . .*

1st ed., London: John Walthoe, 1700. Ralph Asshe-ton* (361).

2nd ed., enlarged, London: John Walthoe, 1719. Jasper Yeates, PLHi.

3rd ed., corrected, London: T. Waller, 1738. Thomas Jefferson, DLC.

8 Barrington, Daines. *Observations upon the statutes, chiefly the more ancient . . . .*[6]

2nd ed., corrected with additions, London: W. Bowyer and J. Nichols, 1766. John Adams, MB.

2nd ed., corrected with additions, London: W. Bowyer and J. Nichols, 1769. Theophilus Parsons* (18).

4th ed., London: W. Bowyer and J. Nichols, 1775. Jasper Yeates, PLHi.

9 Bassett, Thomas. *Catalogue of the Common and Statute Law Books of this Realm.*
William Byrd II* (418); James Grindlay* (282).

10 Beawes, Wyndham. *Lex Mercatoria Rediviva: or, the Merchant's Directory.*
James Grindlay* (281); William Smith, Sr.* (187).

2nd ed., enlarged, London: R. Baldwin and S. Crowder and Co., 1761. Benjamin Chew, PPCl; Thomas Jefferson, DLC.

Revised ed., Thomas Mortimer, ed., London: J. Rivington & Sons, T. Longmans, B. Law, 1783. Jasper Yeates, PLHi.

[6]The title of the fourth edition is *Observations on the more ancient statutes from Magna Carta to the twenty-first of James I, cap. xxvii.*

6th ed., enlarged and improved, Thomas Mortimer, ed., Dublin: J. Rice, 1795. Theophilus Parsons* (18).

11 Blackerby, Samuel. *Cases in Law: Wherein Justices of the Peace have a Jurisdiction . . . .*

London: J. Walthoe, 1717. Benjamin Chew, PPCl; William Smith, Sr.* (188).

12 Blackstone, Sir William. *An Analysis of the Laws of England.*
William Smith, Sr.* (186); St. George Tucker* (77).

Oxford: The Clarendon Press, 1762. Jasper Yeates, PLHi.

13 Blackstone, Sir William. *Commentaries on the Laws of England.*[7]
Francis Dana*; Robert Treat Paine.*

3rd ed., 4 vols., Oxford: The Clarendon Press, 1768–69. John Adams, MB.[8]

4th ed., 4 vols., Oxford: The Clarendon Press, 1770. John Adams, MB;[9] Benjamin Chew, PPCl;[10] Thomas Jefferson, DLC.

5th ed., 4 vols., Oxford: The Clarendon Press, 1773. Theophilus Parsons* (18).

6th ed., 4 vols., Dublin: The Company of Booksellers, 1775. John McClellan, MStOSV.

6th ed., 4 vols., Dublin: The Company of Booksellers, 1783. Theophilus Parsons* (18).

[7]American editions are listed at James, 31, 32, 36, 69, 129.
[8]Vols. 1, 2, and 3 only.
[9]Vol. 4 only.
[10]Vol. 2 only.

11th ed., 4 vols., London: A. Strahan and W. Woodfall, 1791. St. George Tucker, ViW.

14 Blackstone, Sir William. *Law Tracts. Chiefly relating to the Antiquities and Laws of England.*

1st collected ed., 2 vols., Oxford: The Clarendon Press, 1762. John Adams, MB; Thomas Jefferson, DLC; St. George Tucker, ViW.

3rd ed., Oxford: The Clarendon Press, 1771. Jasper Yeates, PLHi.[11]

15 Blount, Thomas. *A Law-Dictionary and Glossary, interpreting such difficult and obscure words and terms, as are found either in our common or statute, ancient or modern, laws.*[12] William Byrd II* (417, 419); Benet Oldham* (407).

3rd ed., William Nelson, ed., London: D. Browne and J. Walthoe, 1717. Thomas Jefferson, DLC.

16 Bohun, William. *Cursus Cancellariae; or, the Course of Proceedings in the High Court of Chancery.*

London: J. Walthoe, 1715. James Alexander* (174); Benjamin Chew, PPCl; James Grindlay* (282); James Logan, PPL; William Smith, Sr.* (186).

2nd ed., corrected and enlarged, London: J. Walthoe, 1723. Jasper Yeates, PLHi.

17 Bohun, William. *Declarations and Pleadings in the most usual Actions brought in the Several Courts of King's Bench and Common Pleas at Westminster.*

[11] Vol. 1 only.

[12] The volume is also known by a variant title, *Νομο-λεξιχον: a Law-Dictionary. Interpreting . . .* , used on the original London edition of 1670.

London: Daniel Browne and John Schuckburgh, 1733. John Mercer* (200); Theophilus Parsons* (18); Jasper Yeates, PLHi.

18 Bohun, William. *The English Lawyer; showing the nature, forms of original writs, process and mandates of the courts at Westminster.*
John Mercer* (201).

1st ed., London: Daniel Browne, John Shuckburgh, and Weaver Bickerton, 1732. Thomas Jefferson, DLC.

19 Bohun, William. *Institutio Legalis: or An introduction to the study and practice of the laws of England, as now regulated and amended by several late statutes.*
Robert Carter* (261); James Grindlay* (282); William Smith, Sr.* (190).

2nd ed., enlarged, London: J. Nutt, 1713. Benjamin Chew, PPCl.

4th ed., corrected and enlarged, London: J. Walthoe, B. Morte, T. Woodward, 1732. Thomas Jefferson, DLC; Jasper Yeates, PLHi.

20 Bohun, William. *Privilegia Londini: or, the rights, liberties, privileges, laws, and customs, of the city of London . . . .*
James Grindlay* (283).

3rd ed., enlarged, London: D. Browne, W. Mears, and R. Gosling, 1723. Thomas Jefferson, DLC.

21 *Book of Oaths and the Severall Forms Thereof, both Antient and Modern.*
James Grindlay* (282); William Smith, Sr.* (190).

22 Booth, George. *The Nature and Practice of Real Actions in their writs and process, both original and judicial . . . .* John Mercer* (200); Robert Treat Paine.*

1st ed., London: Awnsham and John Churchil, 1701. Thomas Jefferson, DLC; Theophilus Parsons* (18); Jasper Yeates, PLHi.

23 Bowman, E. *The English Pleader, Being a Select Collection of Various Precedents of Declarations, pleas and issues.* James Grindlay* (282).

Dublin: James Hoey, 1738. Jasper Yeates, PLHi.

24 Bridgman, Sir Orlando. *Sir Orlando Bridgman's Conveyances: being select precedents of deeds and instruments concerning the most considerable estates in England.* William Byrd II* (417); James Grindlay* (281); Peter Leigh* (256); William Smith, Sr.* (182).

5th ed., enlarged, 2 vols. in 1, London: R. Gosling and Winstanley Battersby, 1725. Thomas Jefferson, DLC.

25 Brown, William. *Clerk's Tutor in Chancery, giving true directions by authentick precedents . . . .* Robert Carter* (147); James Grindlay* (282); William Smith, Sr.* (186).

3rd ed., enlarged, London: H. Morelock, 1705. William Byrd II* (420).

26 Brown, William. *A Compendious and Accurate Treatise of Fines upon writs of covenant; and recoveries upon writs of entry in the post.* William Byrd II* (418); Robert Carter* (148); John Mercer* (200).

2nd ed., corrected and enlarged, London: Abel Roper and Thomas Ward, 1719.[13] Jasper Yeates, PLHi.[14]

5th ed., revised, corrected, and enlarged, London: J. Walthoe, 1718. William Smith, Sr.* (188).

6th ed., revised, corrected, and enlarged, London: D. Browne, J. Walthoe, W. Mears, 1725. Jasper Yeates, PLHi.

27 Brown, William. *Modus Intrandi placita generalia: The Entring Clerk's Introduction.*
William Byrd II* (418); James Grindlay* (282); John Mercer* (200).

3rd ed., corrected, 2 vols., London: J. Walthoe, 1701–1703. Thomas Jefferson, DLC; Jasper Yeates, PLHi.

28 Brown, William. *Praxis Almae Curiae Cancellariae: Being a collection of precedents, by bill and answer, plea and demurrer, in causes of greatest moment (wherein equity hath been allowed) which have been commenced in the High Court of Chancery for more than 30 years last past.*
James Alexander* (174); James Grindlay* (282); John Mercer* (200).

3rd ed., enlarged, 2 vols., London: Abel Roper and Samuel Butler, 1714. Thomas Jefferson, DLC; Jasper Yeates, PLHi.

4th ed., corrected and enlarged, 2 vols., London: E. and R. Nutt, 1725. Benjamin Chew, PPCl.

[13]The second edition was first published in 1684.
[14]Vol. 2 only.

29 Buller, Sir Francis. *An Introduction to the Law Relative to Trials at Nisi Prius.*[15]
Robert Treat Paine*; St. George Tucker* (78).

London: C. Bathurst, 1772. Benjamin Chew, PPCl; Jasper Yeates, PLHi.

3rd ed., corrected, London: C. Bathurst, 1781. Theophilus Parsons* (18).

5th ed., corrected and enlarged, Dublin: Elizabeth Lynch, 1785. John McClellan, MStOSV.

6th ed., corrected and enlarged, Dublin: Elizabeth Lynch, 1791. Thomas Jefferson, DLC.

30 Burn, Richard. *Ecclesiastical Law.*

1st ed., 2 vols., London: H. Woodfall and W. Strahan, 1763–65. Thomas Jefferson, DLC.

2nd ed., 4 vols., London: A. Millar and T. Cadell, 1767. John Adams, MB; Benjamin Chew, PPCl;[16] Theophilus Parsons* (18).

4th ed., 4 vols., London: T. Cadell, 1781. Jasper Yeates, PLHi.

31 Burn, Richard. *The Justice of the Peace and Parish Officer.*
Francis Dana*; Robert Treat Paine.*

7th ed., 3 vols., London: A. Millar, 1762. John Adams, MB;[17] Theophilus Parsons* (18).

11th ed., 4 vols., London: T. Cadell, 1770. Thomas Jefferson, DLC.

[15]For American editions see James, 64.
[16]Vol. 3 only.
[17]Vol. 1 only.

14th ed., enlarged, 4 vols., London: T. Cadell, 1780. Jasper Yeates, PLHi.

32 Burroughs, Samuel. *The History of the Chancery; relating to the Judicial Power of that Court, and the Rights of the Masters . . . .*

London: J. Walthoe, 1726. Thomas Jefferson, DLC; John Mercer* (200).

33 Care, Henry. *English Liberties: Or, The Freeborn subjects inheritance.*[18]
William Byrd II* (420); Robert Treat Paine*; St. George Tucker* (77).

34 Carter, Samuel. *Lex Vadiorum. The Law of Mortgages.*

London: M. Wooton and F. Cogan, 1706. James Alexander* (174); Ralph Assheton* (362); Thomas Jefferson, DLC; William Smith, Sr.* (188); Jasper Yeates, PLHi.

35 Carter, Samuel. *A Treatise concerning Trespasses Vi et Armis. Wherein the nature of trespass is clearly explicated, and the gist of the action stated . . . .*

London: J. Walthoe, 1704. Ralph Assheton* (366); Thomas Jefferson, DLC; Joseph Murray, NNC-L; Jasper Yeates, PLHi.

36 *Clerk's Manual, or, Exact Collections of the Most Approved Forms of Declarations . . . .*

London: 1725. James Grindlay* (282); William Smith, Sr.* (186).

[18]For American editions see James, 5, 46.

37 Clerke, Francis. *The Practice of the Court of Admiralty of England.*[19]

English translation, 1st ed., London: T. Browne and J. Senex, 1722. Thomas Jefferson, DLC; Theophilus Parsons* (19).

38 Clift, Henry. *A New Book of Declarations, Pleadings, Verdicts, Judgements, and Judicial Writs: with entries thereupon . . . .*
Francis Dana*; James Grindlay* (280); William Smith, Sr.* (182).

Sir Charles Ingleby, ed., London: Charles Harper, William Freeman, Timothy Goodwin, 1703. Ralph Assheton* (355); John Mercer* (200); Jasper Yeates, PLHi.

39 Cockburn, William B. *Clerk's Assistant in the Practice of the Ecclesiastical Courts.*
Benet Oldham* (407); William Smith, Sr.* (185).

40 Coke, Sir Edward. *The First Part of the Institutes of the Laws of England. Or, A Commentary upon Littleton . . . .*
James Alexander* (172); William Byrd II* (417, 419); Robert Carter* (149); Francis Dana*; James Grindlay* (280); Benet Oldham* (407); Robert Treat Paine*; William Smith, Sr.* (184).

10th ed., corrected and revised, with the *Compleat Copyholder,* London: William Rawlins and Samuel Roycroft, 1703. Jasper Yeates, PLHi.

11th ed., corrected and enlarged, London: Eliz. Nutt

[19]The title page and text are in Latin and English on facing pages, the Latin title reading *Praxis Curiae admiralitatis angliae.*

and R. Gosling, 1719. Benjamin Chew, PPCl; Theophilus Parsons* (18).

13th ed., corrected and enlarged, Francis Hargrave, ed., London: T. Wright, 1788. Benjamin Chew, PPCl.

13th ed., revised, corrected, and enlarged, with the addition of Francis Hargrave's Notes and References, and a preface and index to the notes by Charles Butler. London: E. Brooke, 1788. Jasper Yeates, PLHi.

41 *The Compleat Clerk in Court; or, Practising Solicitor, in all our courts.*

London: J. Lacy, 1726. Francis Dana*; William Smith, Sr.* (187).

42 *The Compleat Sheriff: wherein is set forth, his office and authority; with directions how and in what manner to execute the same . . . .*

William Smith, Sr.* (190).

London: J. Walthoe, 1718. Benjamin Chew, PPCl.

3rd ed., enlarged, London: J. Walthoe, 1727. John Jay, NNC-L; Thomas Jefferson, DLC.

43 Comyns, Sir John. *A Digest of the Laws of England.*

1st ed., 5 vols., London: John Knapton, Thomas Longman and Robert Horsfield, 1762–67. John Jay, NNC-L.

2nd ed., 5 vols., London: W. Strahan, J. Pote, J. Rivington & Sons. Benjamin Chew, PPCl; Jasper Yeates, PLHi.

3rd ed., 6 vols., London: T. Longman, 1792. Theophilus Parsons* (19).

44 Conset, Henry. *The Practice of the Spiritual or Ecclesiastical Courts.*
James Grindlay* (281); William Smith, Sr.* (186).

3rd ed., corrected and enlarged, London: S. Battersby and J. Walthoe, 1708. Thomas Jefferson, DLC.

45 Cooke, William. *A Compendious System of the Bankrupt Laws.*

Dublin: Lynch, Colles, Burnet, 1786. Theophilus Parsons* (19); Jasper Yeates, PLHi.

46 Cornwall, James. *Tables to the Modern Printed Presidents of Pleadings, Writs, and Returns of Writs, etc., at the Common Law.*

Robert Gardiner, ed., London: Thomas Bever, 1705. Joseph Murray, NNC-L; Jasper Yeates, PLHi.

47 Covert, Nicholas. *The Scrivener's Guide: being choice and approved forms of precedents of all sorts of business now in use and practice . . . .*
Francis Dana*; James Grindlay* (282); Benet Oldham* (407).

4th ed., enlarged, 2 vols., London: E. and R. Nutt, 1724. Benjamin Chew, PPCl.

5th ed., revised, corrected, and enlarged, 2 vols., London: T. Woodward, D. Browne, J. Shuckburgh, C. Hitch and J. Hodges, 1740. Thomas Jefferson, DLC.

48 Cowell, John. *A Law Dictionary: or, The Interpreter of Words and Terms . . . .*[20]

[20]The first edition (1684) bears the title, *Νομοθετης. The Interpreter . . . .*

James Alexander* (173); John Mercer* (200); Robert Treat Paine.*

7th ed., enlarged, London: D. Browne, R. Sare, S. Battersby, J. Walthoe, 1708. Thomas Jefferson, DLC.

Improved, enlarged ed., London: J. Walthoe, B. Lintot, R. Gosling, 1727. John Adams, MB; Jasper Yeates, PLHi.

49 Crompton, George. *Practice common-placed; or the Rules and Cases of Practice in the Courts of King's Bench and Common Pleas, methodically arranged.*

3rd ed., revised and enlarged, 2 vols., London: T. Whieldon, 1786. Jasper Yeates, PLHi.

3rd ed., 2 vols., Dublin: 1787. Theophilus Parsons* (19).

50 Cumberland, Richard. *A Treatise of the Laws of Nature.*

John Maxwell, trans., London: R. Phillips, 1727. Thomas Jefferson, DLC; James Logan* (120); William Smith, Sr.* (187).

51 Cunningham, Timothy. *The Law of Bills of Exchange, Promissory Notes, Bank-Notes and Insurances: containing all the statutes, cases at large . . . methodically digested . . . .*

1st ed., London: W. Owen, 1760. John Mercer* (200).

2nd ed., enlarged, London: W. Owen, 1761. Benjamin Chew, PPCl; Theophilus Parsons* (18).

3rd ed., corrected and enlarged, London: R. Baldwin, W. Owen, and S. Crowder, 1766. Thomas Jefferson, DLC; Jasper Yeates, PLHi.

52 Cunningham, Timothy. *A New and Complete law-dictionary, or, General Abridgement of the Law: on a more extensive plan than any law-dictionary hitherto published.*

1st ed., 2 vols., London: S. Crowder & J. Coote, 1764–65. John Adams, MB; Jasper Yeates, PLHi.

3rd ed., 2 vols., London: J. F. and C. Rivington, T. Longman, S. Crowder, 1783. Thomas Jefferson, DLC.

53 Curson, Henry. *The Law Concerning Estates Taile, and Remainders and Reversions Expectant Thereupon, illustrated.*

London: R. Sare, 1703. Ralph Assheton* (363); Joseph Murray, NNC-L.

54 Dalton, Michael. *The Country Justice: containing the practice of the justices of the peace out of their sessions.*
Robert Carter* (146); Francis Dana*; Robert Treat Paine.*

Reissue of the 1742 ed., enlarged, London: Henry Lintot, 1746. John Adams, MB.

55 Dalton, Michael. *Officium Vicecomitum. The office and authority of sheriffs: gathered out of the statutes, and books of the common laws of this kingdom ....*

London: Richard Atkins and Edward Atkins, 1700. James Alexander* (172); Robert Carter* (146); Francis Dana*; Thomas Jefferson, DLC; William Smith, Sr.* (189).

56 D'Anvers, Knightley. *A General Abridgement of the Common Law, alphabetically digested under proper titles, with notes and references to the whole.*

James Alexander* (173); Robert Carter* (146); James Grindlay* (280); Peter Leigh* (257); John Mercer* (200); William Smith, Sr.* (184, 185).

1st ed., 4 vols., London: John Walthoe, 1705–37.

Ralph Assheton* (356); Benjamin Chew, PPCl;[21] Thomas Jefferson, DLC;[22] Joseph Murray, NNC-L.

2nd ed., corrected, 3 vols., London: J. Walthoe, 1725. Thomas Jefferson, DLC;[23] St. George Tucker, ViW.[24]

2nd ed., corrected, 3 vols., London: J. Walthoe, 1725–37. Jasper Yeates, PLHi.

57 *D[igesti] Justiniani Institutionum libri quatuor. The four books of Justinian's Institutions . . . .*

2nd ed., George Harris, trans., London: M. Withers, 1761. John Jay, NNC-L; Thomas Jefferson, DLC; St. George Tucker, ViW.

58 Domat, Jean. *The Civil law in its Natural Order: together with the publick law.*[25]
James Grindlay* (281); William Smith, Sr.* (182).

1st ed., William Strahan, trans., 2 vols., London: E. Bell, J. Darby and A. Bettesworth, 1722. Ralph Assheton* (361); John Jay, NNC-L; Thomas Jefferson, DLC.

2nd ed., enlarged, William Strahan, trans., 2 vols.,

[21]Vols. 1 and 2 only.

[22]Vol. 3 only.

[23]The first two volumes of the second corrected edition were published in 1725; the third volume, owned by Jefferson, was from the first edition.

[24]Vol. 1 only.

[25]John Adams owned a French edition, *Les loix civiles dans leur ordre naturel,* new ed., corrected and enlarged, Paris: Desprez, 1777.

London: D. Widworth, A. Bettesworth, C. Hitch, G. Strahan, 1737. Jasper Yeates, PLHi.

59 Duncombe, Giles. *Tryals per pais: or, The law of England concerning juries by nisi prius . . . .*
James Alexander* (173); William Byrd II* (418); Benjamin Chew*; Francis Dana*; James Grindlay* (282); John Mercer* (200); Robert Treat Paine.*

8th ed., enlarged, 2 vols., London: T. Waller, 1766. John Adams, MB; Jasper Yeates, PLHi.

60 Fearne, Charles. *An Essay on the Learning of Contingent Remainders and Executory Devises . . . .*
St. George Tucker* (72).

4th ed., revised, corrected, and enlarged, 2 vols., London: Whieldon and Butterworth, 1791–95. Theophilus Parsons* (20).

4th ed., John Joseph Powell, ed., 2 vols., London: J. Butterworth, 1795. Jasper Yeates, PLHi.[26]

5th ed., corrected and revised, London: J. Butterworth, 1795. Jasper Yeates, PLHi.[27]

5th ed., with notes by John Joseph Powell, 2 vols., Dublin: J. Exshaw and J. Rice, 1796. John Adams, MB.

61 Finch, Sir Henry. *Law, or, A discourse thereof; in four books.*
William Byrd II* (418); John Mercer* (201).

Danby Pickering, ed., London: Henry Lintot, 1759. Thomas Jefferson, DLC; Jasper Yeates, PLHi.

[26]Vol. 2 only.
[27]Vol. 1 only.

62 Fitzherbert, Sir Anthony. *The new Natura brevium of the most reverend judge, Mr. Anthony Fitz-Herbert.*
Robert Carter* (147); Francis Dana*; James Grindlay* (282); Peter Leigh* (257); John Mercer* (201); Robert Treat Paine*; St. George Tucker* (74).

Corrected and revised ed., London: Richard and Edward Atkins, 1704. Benjamin Chew, PPCl.

7th ed., corrected, with notes by Lord Chief Justice Matthew Hale, London: R. Gosling, 1730. Theophilus Parsons* (19); William Smith, Sr.* (189).

8th ed., revised and corrected, with notes by Lord Chief Justice Matthew Hale, London: Henry Lintot, 1755. John Adams, MB; Benjamin Chew, PPCl; Jasper Yeats, PLHi.

63 Floyer, Philip. *The Proctor's Practice in the Ecclesiastical Courts.*
James Grindlay* (282); Benet Oldham* (407).

64 Foley, Robert. *Laws Relating to the Poor . . . with cases adjudged in the King's Bench.*

1st ed., London: T. Woodward, 1739. Jasper Yeates, PLHi.

4th ed., London: S. Crowder, 1758. John Adams, MB.

65 Fortescue, Sir John. *De laudibus legum Angliae.*
Robert Carter* (148); Peter Leigh* (257); Benet Oldham* (407).

2nd ed., with notes by John Selden, 3 vols. in 1, London: D. Browne, 1741. John Adams, MB; John Jay, NNC-L; Thomas Jefferson, DLC.

66 Foster, Sir Michael. *A Report of some Proceedings on the Commission of Oyer and Terminer and Goal Delivery for the Trial of the Rebels in the year 1746 in the county of Surry, and of other crown cases. To which are added discourses upon a few branches of the crown law.* St. George Tucker* (78).

Oxford: The Clarendon Press, 1762. John Adams, MB; Jasper Yeates, PLHi.

Dublin: Sarah Cotter, 1767. Thomas Jefferson, DLC.

2nd ed., corrected, London: E. Brooke, 1776. Benjamin Chew, PPCl.

67 Francis, Richard. *Maxims of Equity, Collected from, and proved by Cases, out of the Books of the best Authority, in the High Court of Chancery.* Peter Leigh* (257); John Mercer* (200); William Smith, Sr.* (186).

2nd ed., London: Henry Lintot, 1739. Thomas Jefferson, DLC; Jasper Yeates, PLHi.

68 Gardiner, Robert. *The Doctrine of Demurrers, setting forth variety of Presidents of demurrers in all sorts of actions, and in the several parts of pleadings . . . .*

London: R. Gardiner, 1706. James Alexander* (174); Ralph Assheton* (366); Benjamin Chew, PPCl; William Smith, Sr.* (189).

69 Gardiner, Robert. *Instructor Clericalis. Part I. Directing Clerks both in the Court of King's Bench and Common Pleas . . . .* Robert Treat Paine.*

6th ed., enlarged, London: Thomas Bever, 1721. Benjamin Chew, PPCl; Jasper Yeates, PLHi.

7th ed., enlarged, London: Joel Stephens, 1727. John Adams, MB.

70 Gardiner, Robert. *Instructor Clericalis. Part II. Being a Collection of Choice and Usual Precedents for Declarations in the King's Bench and Common Pleas . . . .*
Robert Treat Paine.*

4th ed., London: T. Bever, 1715. Jasper Yeates, PLHi.

71 Gardiner, Robert. *Instructor Clericalis. Part III. Being a Collection of Choice and Useful Precedents for Pleadings, Both in the King's Bench and Common-Pleas.*
Robert Treat Paine.*

3rd ed., enlarged, London: J. Walthoe, 1713. Benjamin Chew, PPCl; Joseph Murray, NNC-L; Jasper Yeates, PLHi.

4th ed., enlarged, London: J. Walthoe, 1724. John Adams, MB.

72 Gardiner, Robert. *Instructor Clericalis. Part IV. Being a Continuance of Bars and other Pleadings . . . .*
Robert Treat Paine.*

2nd ed., London: John Walthoe and Thos. Bevers, 1717. Joseph Murray, NNC-L; Jasper Yeates, PLHi.

3rd ed., enlarged, London: John Walthoe and Joel Stephens, 1727. John Adams, MB.

73 Gardiner, Robert. *Instructor Clericalis. Part V. Being a Continuance of Bars, and other Pleadings.*
Robert Treat Paine.*

1st ed., 2 vols., London: J. Walthoe, 1713. John Adams, MB; Joseph Murray, NNC-L;[28] Jasper Yeates, PLHi.

2nd ed., 2 vols., corrected, London: E. and R. Nutt, 1722. Benjamin Chew, PPCl.[29]

74 Gardiner, Robert. *The Practick Part of the Law: Shewing the Office of an Attorney, and a Guide to Solicitors . . . .* John Mercer* (200).

4th ed., revised and enlarged, London: John Walthoe, 1711. Jasper Yeates, PLHi.

75 *A General Abridgment of Cases in Equity, argued and adjudged in the High court of chancery . . . .* William Smith, Sr.* (184).

1st ed., 2 vols., London: H. Lintot, 1732–56. Jasper Yeates, PLHi.[30]

4th ed., corrected with notes by Francis Hargrave, 2 vols., London: T. Waller, 1756. Benjamin Chew, PPCl; Thomas Jefferson, DLC; Jasper Yeates, PLHi.[31]

5th ed., London: A. Strahan and W. Woodfall, 1769. John Jay, NNC-L.

76 *A General Treatise of Naval Trade and Commerce, as founded on the laws and statutes of this realm . . . .* James Grindlay* (282); John Mercer* (200); Robert Treat Paine.*

[28]Vol. 1 only.
[29]Vol. 2 only.
[30]Vol. 1 only.
[31]Vol. 2 only. The 1756 printing consisted of the fourth edition of Vol. 1 and the first edition of Vol. 2.

1st ed., 2 vols., London: Edward Symon, 1740. John Adams, MB.[32]

2nd ed., enlarged, 2 vols., London: J. Brotherton, 1753. John Adams, MB;[33] Thomas Jefferson, DLC.

77 Gibson, Edmund. *Codex Juris Ecclesiastici Anglicani: or, the Statutes, Constitutions, Canons, Rubricks, and Articles of the Church of England . . . .*

1st ed., 2 vols., London: R. Whitledge, 1713. Thomas Jefferson, DLC.

2nd ed., 2 vols., Oxford: The Clarendon Press, 1761. Jasper Yeates, PLHi.

78 Gilbert, Sir Geoffrey. *The History and Practice of the Court of Common Pleas.*[34]
Benet Oldham* (407); St. George Tucker* (78).

1st ed., London: C. Ward and R. Chandler, 1737. Benjamin Chew, PPCl.

3rd ed., corrected and enlarged, London: P. Uriel and E. Brooke, 1779. Jasper Yeates, PLHi.

79 Gilbert, Sir Geoffrey. *The Law of Devises, Revocations and Last Wills. To which is added choice precedents of wills.*
James Grindlay* (281).

4th ed., revised, corrected, and improved, Dublin: J. Moore, 1792. Theophilus Parsons* (20).

80 Gilbert, Sir Geoffrey. *The Law of Distresses and Replevins, delineated.*

[32]Vol. 1 only.
[33]Vol. 1 only.
[34]The title of the third edition is *The History and Practice of Civil Actions, Particularly in the Court of Common Pleas . . . .*

Benet Oldham* (407).

London: J. Worrall and B. Tovey, 1757. Thomas Jefferson, DLC; Theophilus Parsons* (20).

2nd ed., enlarged, London: Edward Brooke, 1780. Jasper Yeates, PLHi.

81 Gilbert, Sir Geoffrey. *The Law of Evidence.*[35]
James Grindlay* (282).

Dublin: Sarah Cotter, 1754. Benjamin Chew, PPCl.

2nd ed., corrected, London: W. Owen, 1760. Benjamin Chew, PPCl.

3rd ed., corrected and enlarged, London: W. Owen, 1769. John McClellan, MStOSV.

4th ed., corrected and enlarged, London: J. F. and C. Rivington, W. Owen, 1777. Jasper Yeates, PLHi.

Enlarged ed., Capel Lofft, ed., 4 vols. in 2, Dublin: P. Byrne, 1795–97. Theophilus Parsons* (20).

82 Gilbert, Sir Geoffrey. *The Law of Uses and Trusts: collected and digested in a proper order . . . .*
John Mercer* (200).

1st ed., London: R. Gosling, 1734. Thomas Jefferson, DLC.

83 Gilbert, Sir Geoffrey. *A Treatise of Tenures.*

Dublin: Sarah Cotter, 1754. Jasper Yeates, PLHi.

3rd ed., enlarged, London: D. Browne, J. Worrall and A. Millar, 1757. Benjamin Chew, PPCl; Thomas Jefferson, DLC; Theophilus Parsons* (20); St. George Tucker, ViW.

[35] American editions are listed at James, 65.

84 Godolphin, John. *The Orphan's Legacy: or, A Testamentary Abridgement.*
James Alexander* (173); William Byrd II* (418); Robert Carter* (147); Robert Treat Paine.*

4th ed., enlarged, London: Robert Vincent, 1701. John Adams, MB; Thomas Jefferson, DLC.

85 Goguet, Antoine Yves, and Fugere, Alexander C. *The Origin of Laws, Arts, and Sciences, and their progress among the most ancient nations.*
William Smith, Sr.* (182); St. George Tucker* (77).

3 vols., Edinburgh: G. Robinson, 1775.[36] John Adams, MB.

86 Goodinge, Thomas. *The Law against Bankrupts.*
James Grindlay* (282).

2nd ed., enlarged, London: John Hartley, 1701. Thomas Jefferson, DLC.

87 Greenwood, William. *The Authority, Jurisdiction and Method of Keeping County-courts, Courts-leet, and Courts-baron. Explaining the judicial and ministerial authority of sheriffs.*[37]
James Alexander* (174); William Byrd II* (418); James Grindlay* (282).

8th ed., enlarged, London: D. Browne and J. Walthoe, 1722. Thomas Jefferson, DLC.

[36]This would appear to be a second printing of the first edition of 1761.

[37]The first eighteenth-century edition, that of 1722, bears this title. Seventeenth-century printings of this book bore the title, *Βουλευτηριον; or, A practical demonstration of county-judicatures . . . .*

88 Grotius, Hugo. *De Jure Belli Ac Pacis libri tres, in quibus jus nature & gentium, item juris publici praecipua explicantur.* James Alexander* (173); William Byrd II* (420).

New ed., Amsterdam: Janssonio-Waesbergios, 1712. James Logan, PPL.

89 Grotius, Hugo. *Of the Rights of War and Peace; in which are explain'd the laws and claims of nature and nations, and the principal points that relate either to publick government, or the conduct of private life ....* William Byrd II* (419, 420); William Smith, Sr.* (183).

Jean Barbeyrac, ed., 3 vols. in 1, London: W. Innys and R. Manby, J. and P. Knapton, D. Osborn, and E. Wicksteed, 1738.[38] John Adams, MB; Benjamin Chew, PPCl; James Logan, PPL.

90 Hale, Sir Matthew. *De Successionibus apud Anglos: The Law of Hereditary Descents.* John Mercer* (201).

London: S.S., 1700. Jasper Yeates, PLHi.

91 Hale, Sir Matthew. *The History and Analysis of the Common Law of England; written by a learned hand ....*[39] William Byrd II* (419); Benet Oldham* (407).

1st ed., London: J. Walthoe, 1713. Ralph Assheton*

[38]Thomas Jefferson's library contained a French translation by Barbeyrac, published in 1724.

[39]There are two variants of this title in imprints of slightly different sizes. The title used here is composed of 264 pages and is 20 centimeters in size; the other title, *The history of the common law of England,* 264 pages and 18½ centimeters, contains *The analysis of the law* within the same volume. This shorter form of the title was used on the third edition, which also contains *The Analysis of the Law.*

(366); John Mercer* (200); St. George Tucker* (78).
3rd ed., corrected, 2 vols. in 1, London: T. Waller, 1739. Thomas Jefferson, DLC.

92 Hale, Sir Matthew. *Historia Placitorum Coronae. The History of the Pleas of the Crown . . . .*
Peter Leigh* (257).

1st ed., 2 vols., London: F. Gyles, T. Woodward, and C. Davis, 1736. John Adams, MB; Benjamin Chew, PPCl; James Grindlay* (280); John Jay, NNC-L; John Mercer* (200); Theophilus Parsons* (20); William Smith, Sr.* (183); St. George Tucker, ViW; Jasper Yeates, PLHi.

New ed., corrected and revised, George Wilson, ed., 2 vols., London: T. Payne, P. Uriel, 1778. Thomas Jefferson, DLC.

93 Hale, Sir Matthew. *Pleas of the Crown; or, A Methodical Summary of the Principal Matters relating to that Subject.*
James Alexander* (174).

5th ed., enlarged, London: D. Brown, J. Walthoe, M. Wotton, 1716. John Jay, NNC-L; Thomas Jefferson, DLC; Jasper Yeates, PLHi.

94 Hargrave, Francis. *Collecteana Juridica; Consisting of Tracts Relative to the Law and Constitution of England.*

2 vols., London: E. and R. Brooke, 1791–92. Theophilus Parsons* (19); Jasper Yeates, PLHi.[40]

95. Hargrave, Sir Francis. *A Collection of tracts relative to the Law of England . . . .*

[40]Vol. 1 only.

St. George Tucker* (78).

1st ed., Dublin: E. Lynch, W. Colles, 1787. Theophilus Parsons* (20).

1st ed., London: E. Brooke, 1787. Jasper Yeates, PLHi.[41]

96 Harrison, Joseph. *The Accomplish'd Practiser in the High court of chancery, showing the whole method of proceedings, according to the present practice, from the bill to the appeal inclusive* . . . .
James Grindlay* (282); Benet Oldham* (407); St. George Tucker* (78).

7th ed., revised and enlarged, with notes by John Griffith Williams, 2 vols., London: T. Whieldon & R. Pheney, 1790. Jasper Yeates, PLHi.

97 Hawkins, William. *An Abridgment of the First Part of my Lord Coke's Institutes; with some additions explaining many of the difficult cases, and shewing in what points the law has been altered by late resolutions and acts of Parliament.*
James Grindlay* (282); Robert Treat Paine.*

5th ed., enlarged, London: T. Osborne, 1736. Jasper Yeates, PLHi.

7th ed., enlarged, London: D. Browne, J. Shuckburgh, 1751. Thomas Jefferson, DLC.

98 Hawkins, William. *A Treatise of the Pleas of the Crown: or, A system of the principal matters relating to that subject, digested under proper heads* . . . .
Francis Dana*; Thomas Jefferson* (294); Peter Leigh*

[41]Vol. 1 only.

(257); Benet Oldham* (407); Robert Treat Paine*; William Smith, Sr.* (184).

1st ed., 2 vols. in 1, London: J. Walthoe and J. Walthoe, Jr., 1716–21. Ralph Assheton* (360); Joseph Murray, NNC-L.

4th ed., enlarged, 2 vols. in 1, London: D. Browne, J. Worrall, A. Shuckburgh, 1762. John Adams, MB; Jasper Yeates, PLHi.

5th ed., enlarged, London: J. Worrall and Co., 1771. Theophilus Parsons* (20).

99 Heath, Sir Robert. *Maxims and Rules of Pleading in Actions, Real, Personal and Mixd, Popular and Penal . . . .*

London: His Majesty's Law Printers, 1771. Benjamin Chew, PPCl; Theophilus Parsons* (20).

100 Heineccius, Johannes G. *A Methodical System of Universal Law: or, The Laws of Nature and of Nations.*

George Turnbull, ed., 2 vols., London: J. Noon, 1741. John Adams, MB; Jasper Yeates, PLHi.

101 Highmore, Anthony, Jr. *A Digest of the Doctrine of Bail in Civil and Criminal Causes.*

1st ed., London: T. Cadell, 1783. Jasper Yeates, PLHi.

Dublin: 1791. Theophilus Parsons* (20).

102 Hinde, Robert. *The Modern Practice of the High Court of Chancery . . . .*

Dublin: E. Lynch, G. Burnett, W. Colles, 1786. Thomas Jefferson, DLC; Jasper Yeates, PLHi.

103 Horne, Andrew. *Mirrour of Justices.*

W. H., trans., London: J. Worrall and B. Tovey, 1768. St. George Tucker, ViW; Jasper Yeates, PLHi.

104 Horsman, Gilbert. *Precedents in Conveyancing.* James Grindlay* (280).

1st ed., 2 vols., London: John and Paul Knapton, 1744. Thomas Jefferson, DLC.

3rd ed., 4 vols., Dublin: Sarah Cotter, 1764. Jasper Yeates, PLHi.

105 Impey, John. *The New Instructor Clericalis, stating the Authority, Jurisdiction, and Modern Practice of the Court of King's Bench.*

2nd ed., enlarged, London: J. Impey, 1785. Benjamin Chew, PPCl.

2nd ed., corrected, London: John Impey, 1786. Jasper Yeates, PLHi.

4th ed., enlarged, London: J. Impey, 1788. Jasper Yeates, PLHi.

5th ed., corrected, London: J. Impey, 1791. Theophilus Parsons* (20).

106 *Infant's Lawyer; or, Law, both ancient and modern, Relating to Infants, with appendix of forms.*[42] Benet Oldham* (407); William Smith, Sr.* (187).

3rd ed., London: James Crokatt, 1726. Jasper Yeates, PLHi.

[42]The title of the third edition is *Infant's lawyer: or law (Ancient and Modern) Relating to Infants.*

107 Jacob, Giles. *The Common Law Common-placed. . . .*

1st ed., London: W. Mears, T. Corbett, and J. Hooke, 1726. Thomas Jefferson, DLC; William Smith, Sr.* (187).

108 Jacob, Giles. *Every Man his own Lawyer; or, Summary of the laws of England . . . .*[43]
John Mercer* (200).

7th ed., Dublin: 1776. John McClellan, MStOSV.

109 Jacob, Giles. *Law Grammar; or Rudiments of the law.*
Benet Oldham* (407); Robert Treat Paine.*

110 Jacob, Giles.[44] *Law Quibbles: or a Treatise of the Evasions, Tricks, Turns and Quibbles, commonly used in the Profession of Law, to the Prejudice of Clients, and others.*
James Grindlay* (282); John Mercer* (200).

1st ed., London: T. Corbett, 1724. James Logan, PPL.

111 Jacob, Giles. *Lex Mercatoria; or, The merchant's companion; containing all the laws and statutes relating to merchandize . . . .*
James Alexander* (172); Robert Carter* (149); William Smith, Sr.* (183).

1st ed., London: E. Gurll, 1718. Joseph Murray, NNC-L.

2nd ed., corrected and enlarged, London: B. Motte, J. Clarke, J. Lacy, 1729. Ralph Assheton* (355); John Jay, NNC-L; Thomas Jefferson, DLC.

[43]For American editions see James, 27, 28.

[44]The attribution follows that of Edwin Wolf 2nd, in *The Library of James Logan of Philadelphia 1674–1751* (Philadelphia, 1974), 252.

112 Jacob, Giles. *A New Law-dictionary: containing, the interpretation and definition of words and terms used in the law ....*[45]
Francis Dana*; James Grindlay* (281); John Mercer* (200); Benet Oldham* (407); Robert Treat Paine*; William Smith, Sr.* (182); St. George Tucker* (70).

3rd ed., enlarged, London: J.J. and P. Knapton, 1736. Theophilus Parsons* (21).

4th ed., corrected and enlarged., London: D. Midwinter, R. Ware, C. Rivington, A. Ward, J. and P. Knapton, 1739. James Logan, PPL.

London: R. Ware, 1743.[46] John Adams, MB.

8th ed., revised and enlarged, London: T. Osborne, C. Hitch, L. Hawes, 1762. Jasper Yeates, PLHi.

10th ed., corrected and enlarged, J. Morgan, ed., London: W. Strahan, J. Rivington and Sons, 1782. Benjamin Chew, PPCl.

113 Jacob, Giles. *The Statute-law Common-plac'd: or, A second general table to the statutes.*[47]
James Grindlay* (282); Peter Leigh* (257); Benet Oldham* (407); William Smith, Sr.* (189).

5th ed., revised, London: Henry Lintot, 1748. St. George Tucker, ViW.

[45]The title as given is from the third edition. The first edition imprint of 1729 is entitled, *The Law-dictionary: explaining the rise, progress, and present state of the English law ....*

[46]The title of this edition deletes the words "used in the law."

[47]This title, issued in 1719, 1730, 1731, and 1739, appears to be a supplement to Jacob's *A review of the statutes, both ancient and modern; ... With an exact table to the whole,* published in 1713. A copy of the 1713 imprint is in Thomas Jefferson, DLC.

114 Jones, Sir William. *An Essay on the Law of Bailments.*[48]
Robert Treat Paine.*

Dublin: Henry Watts, 1790. Jasper Yeates, PLHi.

115 *Jus Imperii & Servitutis; or, Law concerning Masters, Apprentices, Bayliffs, Receivers, Stewards, Attorneys, etc.*

London: 1707. James Alexander* (174); Francis Dana*; John Mercer* (200).

116 Justice, Alexander. *A General Treatise of the Dominion and Laws of the Sea.*
John Mercer* (200).

1st ed., London: S. and J. Sprint, 1705. Theophilus Parsons* (23).
2nd ed., enlarged, London: J. Nicholson, 1709. John Jay, NNC-L.
3rd ed., enlarged, London: Executors of J. Nicholson, 1710. Thomas Jefferson, DLC.

117 Kames, Henry Home, Lord. *Essays upon Several Subjects concerning British antiquities; viz. I. Introduction of the feudal law into Scotland. II. Constitution of Parliament. III. Honour, Dignity. IV. Succession or descent.*

3rd ed., enlarged, Edinburgh: A. Kincaid and J. Bell, 1763. John Adams, MB; Thomas Jefferson, DLC; St. George Tucker, ViW.

118 Kames, Henry Home, Lord. *Historical Law-tracts.*
St. George Tucker* (70).

2nd ed., Edinburgh: A. Kincaid and J. Bell, 1761. John Adams, MB; Thomas Jefferson, DLC.

[48]For American editions see James, 112.

119 Kames, Henry Home, Lord. *Principles of Equity.*

1st ed., Edinburgh: A. Millar, A. Kincaid and J. Bell, 1760. Thomas Jefferson, DLC.

2nd ed., corrected and enlarged, Edinburgh: A. Millar, A. Kincaid and J. Bell, 1767. Thomas Jefferson, DLC; Jasper Yeates, PLHi.

3rd ed., 2 vols., Edinburgh: J. Bell, W. Creech, T. Cadell, 1778. Thomas Jefferson, DLC.

120 Kilburne, Richard. *Choice Presidents upon all Acts of Parliament Relating to the Office and Duty of a Justice of the Peace . . . .*
William Byrd II* (418); Francis Dana.*

121 Kyd, Stewart. *A Treatise on the Law of Bills of Exchange and Promissory Notes.*[49]
Robert Treat Paine.*

1st ed., Dublin: G. Burnet, E. Lynch, P. Wogan, 1791. Jasper Yeates, PLHi.

3rd ed., London: J. Johnson, 1795. John Adams, MB; Theophilus Parsons* (20).

122 *The Law of Actions on the Case for Torts and Wrongs . . . .*

London: T. Tyre, 1741. Thomas Jefferson, DLC; Joseph Murray, NNC-L.

123 *The Law of Commons and Commoners; or, A treatise showing the original and nature of common, and the several kinds thereof . . . .*

2nd ed., corrected and enlarged, London: John

[49]For American editions see James, 126, 127, 138.

Walthoe, 1720. Thomas Jefferson, DLC; William Smith, Sr.* (190).

124 *The Law of Corporations: containing the Laws and Customs of all the Corporations and Inferior Courts of Record in England.*

London: I. Cleeve, 1702. James Alexander* (173); Benjamin Chew, PPCl; James Grindlay* (282); John Jay, NNC-L.

125 *The Law of Covenants; a Treatise explaining the Nature and Rules of the several Sorts of Covenants . . . .*
James Alexander* (174); William Smith, Sr.* (186).

1st ed., London: S. Butler, 1711. Ralph Assheton* (363); Jasper Yeates, PLHi.

2nd ed., London: Samuel Butler, 1712. Thomas Jefferson, DLC.

126 *The Law of Ejectments, or, A treatise shewing the nature of ejectione firme . . . .*
James Alexander* (174); James Grindlay* (282); Peter Leigh* (257); John Mercer* (201); William Smith, Sr.* (189).

1st ed., London: John Deebe, 1700. Ralph Assheton* (362); Thomas Jefferson, DLC; Jasper Yeates, PLHi.

2nd ed., enlarged, London: J. Walthoe, 1713. Benjamin Chew, PPCl; Theophilus Parsons* (21).

127 *The Law of Errors and Writs of Error.*

London: I. Cleave, 1703. Ralph Assheton* (362); James Grindlay* (282); John Jay, NNC-L; William Smith, Sr.* (187).

128 *The Law of Executors and Administrators. Being a common law treatise; shewing, directions for the management of their office and duty, in the several branches of it.* Benet Oldham* (407).

London: J. Walthoe, 1701. James Alexander* (173); Ralph Assheton* (361).

London: J. Walthoe, 1702. Joseph Murray, NNC-L.

129 *The Law of Executions: or, A treatise shewing and explaining the nature of executions . . . .*[50]

London: R. Battersby, 1706. James Alexander* (174); Benjamin Chew, PPCl; William Smith, Sr.* (186).

130 *The Law-French Dictionary alphabetically digested; very useful for all young students in the common laws of England. To which is added, The law-Latin dictionary. . . .*

London: Isaac Cleave and John Hartley, 1701. Ralph Assheton* (362).

2nd ed., corrected and enlarged, 2 vols. in 1, London: D. Browne, J. Walthoe, B. Tooke, 1718. John Adams, MB; John Mercer* (200); Theophilus Parsons* (20); William Smith, Sr.* (189); Jasper Yeates, PLHi.

131 *The Laws of England Delineated.*

London: Thomas Wooton, 1729. Thomas Jefferson, DLC; William Smith, Sr.* (187, 190).

132 Levinz, Sir Creswell. *A Collection of Select and Modern Entries of declarations, pleadings, verdicts, judgements, etc. . . .*

[50]The title has been attributed to Samuel Carter but is customarily cited by title alone.

London: D. Browne, T. Benskin, J. Walthoe, 1702. Francis Dana*; Thomas Jefferson, DLC; Peter Leigh* (257); Theophilus Parsons* (21); William Smith, Sr.* (182).

133 Lilly, John. *A Collection of Modern Entries, being a collection of select pleadings in the courts of King's bench, Common pleas and Exchequer . . . .*[51]
Benjamin Chew*; Francis Dana*; James Grindlay* (281); John Mercer* (200); Robert Treat Paine.*

1st ed., London: D. Browne, W. Mears, R. Gosling, 1723. John Adams, MB; William Smith, Sr.* (182); St. George Tucker* (76).

3rd ed., enlarged, London: D. Browne, T. Osborne, J. Worrall, 1758. Jasper Yeates, PLHi.

6th ed., 2 vols., Dublin: Burnett, 1792. Theophilus Parsons* (21).

134 Lilly, John. *A Continuation of the Practical Register, in two Parts.*

2 vols., London: Charles Harper, 1710. Benjamin Chew, PPCl; Jasper Yeates, PLHi.

135 Lilly, John. *The Practical Conveyancer: in Two Parts.*

London: Thomas Ward and John Hooke, 1719. Benjamin Chew, PPCl; Francis Dana*; Thomas Jefferson, DLC; Robert Treat Paine*; William Smith, Sr.* (184).

136 Lilly, John. *The Practical Register: or, A General Abridgment of the Laws . . . .*

[51]The third and subsequent editions are entitled *A Collection of Modern Entries; or, Select pleadings in the Courts of King's Bench, and Exchequer . . . .*

James Alexander* (173); Francis Dana*; James Grindlay* (280); William Smith, Sr.* (183).

1st ed., 2 vols., London: T. Ward, 1719. Ralph Assheton* (360, 362); Joseph Murray, NNC-L.

2nd ed., enlarged, 2 vols., London: J. Walthoe, 1735. Thomas Jefferson, DLC.

2nd ed., enlarged, 2 vols., London: J. Shuckburgh, 1745. Jasper Yeates, PLHi.

137 de Lolme, Jean Louis. *The Constitution of England, or, an Account of the English government; In which it is compared, both with the Republican Form of Government, and the other Monarchies in Europe.*
St. George Tucker* (78).

4th ed., corrected and enlarged, London: G. Robinson and J. Murray, 1784. Benjamin Chew, PPCl; Theophilus Parsons* (19); Jasper Yeates, PLHi.

138 Macclesfield, Thomas Parker, Earl of. *The Tryal of Thomas Earl of Macclesfield, in the House of Peers, for high crimes and misdemeanors; upon impeachment . . . .*

London: S. Buckley, 1725. Thomas Jefferson, DLC; William Smith, Sr.* (181).

139 Mallory, John. *The Attorney's Pocket Companion: or, A guide to the practisers of the law . . . .*
James Grindlay* (282).

2nd ed., corrected, 2 vols. in 1, London: R. Gosling, 1733. Benet Oldham* (407).

2nd ed., 2 vols. in 1, London and Dublin: Sam Fairbrother, 1734. William Smith, Sr.* (190).

3rd ed., 2 vols. in 1, London: E. and R. Nutt and R. Gosling, 1759. St. George Tucker, ViW.

140 Mallory, John. *Modern Entries, in English: Being a Select Collection of Pleadings in the Courts of King's Bench, Common Pleas and Exchequer . . . .*
James Grindlay* (280); Robert Treat Paine.*

4th ed., enlarged, 2 vols., Dublin: H. Watts, 1791. Theophilus Parsons* (21).

141 Mallory, John. *Quare Impedit. In two parts: (I) containing an Abridgment of the Law Concerning the Patronage of Churches, the titles of Ecclesiastical Persons to their Estates, the manner of conveying, granting and leasing them, etc. (II) containing Precedents of Pleadings.*

London: E. and R. Nutt and R. Gosling, 1737. Peter Leigh* (257); John Mercer* (200).

142 Millar, John, Jr. *Elements of the Law relating to Insurances.*

Edinburgh: J. Bell and G. G. & J. Robinson, 1787. Theophilus Parsons* (21); Jasper Yeates, PLHi.

143 *Modern Conveyancer; or, Conveyancing improved.*
James Grindlay* (282); William Smith, Sr.* (190).

2nd ed., corrected, 2 vols., London: J. Walthoe, 1716. Joseph Murray, NNC-L.

144 Molloy, Charles. *De Jure Maritimo et Navali: or, A Treatise of Affairs Maritime and of Commerce . . . .*
James Alexander* (173); William Byrd II* (419); Robert Carter* (147); Francis Dana*; Robert Treat Paine*; William Smith, Sr.* (186).

7th ed., enlarged, London: John Walthoe, Jr., and J. Wotton, 1722. Thomas Jefferson, DLC.

8th ed., enlarged, London: J. Walthoe, 1744. John Adams, MB.

9th ed., enlarged with notes by Francis Hargrave, 2 vols., London: T. Waller, 1769. John Jay, NNC-L; Theophilus Parsons* (21); St. George Tucker* (74); Jasper Yeates, PLHi.

145 Morgan, John. *The Attorney's Vade Mecum, and Client's Instructor . . . .*

3 vols. in 2, Dublin: G. Burney, E. Lynch, J. Moore, 1792. Theophilus Parsons* (21); Jasper Yeates, PLHi.

146 Nelson, William. *An Abridgment of the Common Law: being a collection of the principal cases argued and adjudged in the several courts of Westminster-hall.*

3 vols., London: R. Gosling, W. Mears, 1725–26. John Adams, MB;[52] Robert Carter* (147); James Grindlay* (281); Thomas Jefferson, DLC; Peter Leigh* (257); Robert Treat Paine*; St. George Tucker, ViW.

147 Nelson, William. *The Law of Evidence: Wherein All the Cases that have yet been printed in any of our law books or tryals, and that in any wise relate to points of evidence, are collected and methodically digested . . . .*
William Smith, Sr.* (186).

1st ed., London: R. Gosling, 1717. Ralph Assheton* (361); Thomas Jefferson, DLC; Jasper Yeates, PLHi.

[52]Vol. 1 only.

148 Nelson, William. *Lex Testamentaria: or, a Compendious System of all the Laws of England, as well before the statute of Henry VIII. as since, concerning last wills and testaments.*
Francis Dana*; James Grindlay* (282); John Mercer* (201); William Smith, Sr.* (186).

1st ed., London: T. Bever, 1714. James Alexander* (173); Ralph Assheton* (361).

2nd ed., corrected and enlarged, London: J. Stephens, 1724. John Jay, NNC-L; Theophilus Parsons* (22); St. George Tucker, ViW.

2nd ed., corrected and enlarged, London: J. Stephens, 1728. Thomas Jefferson, DLC.

149 Nelson, William. *The Office and Authority of a Justice of the Peace: Collected out of all the Books, whether of Common or Statute Law, hitherto written on that Subject.*
Francis Dana.*

7th ed., corrected and enlarged, London: D. Browne, J. Walthoe, B. Tooke, 1721. James Logan, PPL.

11th ed., 2 vols., corrected and enlarged, London: R. Gosling, W. Mears, T. Woodward, 1736. Thomas Jefferson, DLC.

150 Noodt, Gerard. *Opera omnia juridica, cum ejusdem vita a Joan. Barbeyracio.*

2 vols. in 1, Leiden: E. Luzac, 1760. John Adams, MB.

2 vols., Leiden: Theodore Haak, 1767. Thomas Jefferson, DLC.[53]

[53]Vol. 1 only.

151 *Of Last Wills and Testaments: A Common-Law Treatise, containing several rules for the construction of last wills, and the diversities between limitations and conditions in a will.*

London: J. Walthoe, 1703. James Alexander* (173); Ralph Assheton* (362).

152 *Officium Clerici Pacis: A Book of Indictments, Informations, Inquisitions and Appeals . . . .*
James Alexander* (174); Francis Dana*; James Grindlay* (282).

2nd ed., enlarged, London: D. Browne and J. Walthoe, 1705. Benjamin Chew, PPCl; Thomas Jefferson, DLC; Joseph Murray, NNC-L; Theophilus Parsons* (22).

3rd ed., enlarged, London: D. Browne and J. Walthoe, 1726. John Jay, NNC-L; Jasper Yeates, PLHi.

153 Park, Sir James Alan. *A System of the Law of Marine Insurances.*[54]
Robert Treat Paine.*

1st ed., London: T. Whieldon, 1787. Theophilus Parsons* (22); Jasper Yeates, PLHi.

154 Pigott, Nathaniel. *New Precedents in Conveyancing: containing great variety of curious draughts, many of them on special occasions . . . .*

London: J. Worrall, 1742. John Adams, MB; Thomas Jefferson, DLC.

155 Pigott, Nathaniel. *A Treatise of Common Recoveries, their Nature and Use.*

[54]For American editions see James, 66, 132, 135.

1st ed., London: J. Shuckburgh, 1739. Joseph Murray, NNC-L.

2nd ed., corrected and revised, London: J. Worrall & B. Tovey, and P. Uriel, 1770. Jasper Yeates, PLHi.

156 *Pleader's Assistant; containing a select collection of precedents of modern pleadings, in the courts of King's bench and common pleas, etc. . . .*

Dublin: Lynch, McKenzie, Davis, and Jones, 1786. John McClellan, MStOSV.

Dublin: 1795. Theophilus Parsons* (22).

157 Plowden, Edmund. *The Commentaries or Reports of Edmund Plowden . . . containing diverse cases upon matters of law . . . To which are added, the quaeries of Mr. Plowden . . . .* James Grindlay* (281).

Enlarged ed., London: Catherine Lintot and Samuel Richardson, 1761. John Adams, MB; Thomas Jefferson, DLC.

158 *The Pocket Conveyancer, or, Attorney's Useful Companion . . . .*

1st ed., 2 vols., London: G. Kearsley, 1760. Jasper Yeates, PLHi.

2nd ed., 2 vols., London: 1773. Theophilus Parsons* (22).

159 Powell, John Joseph. *An Essay on the Learning respecting the Creation and Execution of Powers . . . .*

1st ed., London: P. Uriel and T. Whieldon, 1787. Jasper Yeates, PLHi.

2nd ed., corrected and enlarged, J. Butterworth, 1799. Theophilus Parsons* (22).

160 Powell, John Joseph. *Essay upon the Law of Contracts and Agreements.*
Robert Treat Paine.*

2 vols., London: 1790. Theophilus Parsons* (22).

2 vols. in 1, Dublin: Chamberlaine and Rice, 1790. John McClellan, MStOSV; Jasper Yeates, PLHi.

2 vols. in 1, Dublin: P. Byrne, J. Moore, 1796. John Adams, MB.

161 Powell, John Joseph. *An Essay upon the learning of Devises . . . .*
St. George Tucker* (71).

1st ed., London: P. Uriel, J. Johnson and T. Whieldon, 1788. Theophilus Parsons* (22); Jasper Yeates, PLHi.

162 Powell, John Joseph. *A Treatise upon the Law of Mortgages.*

2nd ed., London: P. Uriel and T. Whieldon, 1787. Jasper Yeates, PLHi.

3rd ed., London: 1791. Theophilus Parsons* (22).

163 *The Practical Register in Chancery: or, A Compleat Collection of the Standing Orders and Rules of Practice in Chancery.*

London: D. Brown, W. Mears, J. Brown, 1714. James Alexander* (174); James Grindlay* (282); Thomas Jefferson, DLC; Jasper Yeates, PLHi.

164 *Precedents in Chancery, being a Collection of Cases Argued and Adjudged in the High Court of Chancery . . . 1689, to 1722 . . . .*

1st ed., London: Arthur Bettelworth and Charles Hitch, 1733. Jasper Yeates, PLHi.

2nd ed., enlarged, London: Henry Lintot, 1750. Benjamin Chew, PPCl.

165 von Pufendorf, Samuel, Baron. *De Officio Hominis & Civis juxta Legem Naturalem Libri Duo.*
William Byrd II* (418).

2nd ed., revised, Thomas Johnson, ed., London: Knapton, Innys, Wallant, 1737. James Logan, PPL.
3rd ed., corrected and revised, Thomas Johnson, ed., 2 vols. in 1, London: I. Beecroft, P. Vaillant & I. Nourse, 1748. Jasper Yeates, PLHi.

166 von Pufendorf, Samuel, Baron. *Le Droit de la nature et des gens . . . .*
William Smith, Sr.* (187).

New revised and enlarged ed., Jean Barbeyrac, trans., 3 vols., London: Jean Nours, 1740. Thomas Jefferson, DLC.

167 von Pufendorf, Samuel, Baron. *Of the Law of Nature and Nations.*
William Byrd II* (419); James Grindlay* (281); Benet Oldham* (407).

English ed., Basil Kennett and William Percivale, trans., Oxford: A. and J. Churchil, R. Sare, H. Bonwick, 1703. James Logan, PPL.
4th ed., corrected, Basil Kennett, trans., London: J. Walthoe, R. Wilkins, J. & J. Bonwick, 1729. John Adams, MB; John Jay, NNC-L; St. George Tucker* (70); Jasper Yeates, PLHi.
5th ed., Basil Kennet, trans., London: J. & J. Bonwicke, 1749. Thomas Jefferson, DLC.

168 Rastell, John. *Les Terms de la Ley: or, Certaine Difficult and Obscure Words, and Termes of the Common Lawes of this Realm expounded.*[55]
William Byrd II* (418); Robert Carter* (147); John Mercer* (200).

Corrected and enlarged ed., London: R. Gosling, 1721. Jasper Yeates, PLHi.[56]

169 *Readings upon the Statute Law. Alphabetically Digested . . . .*

5 vols., London: The author, printed by D. Browne, T. Osborne, W. Mears, 1723–25. James Grindlay* (282); Joseph Murray, NNC-L;[57] Jasper Yeates, PLHi.[58]

170 Redesdale, John Freeman-Mitford, Baron. *A Treatise of the Pleadings in Suits in the Court of Chancery by English Bill.*[59]

1st ed., London: W. Owen, 1780. Thomas Jefferson* (200).

1st ed., Dublin: 1781. Theophilus Parsons* (21).

2nd ed., London: W. Owen, 1787. Jasper Yeates, PLHi.

2nd ed., Dublin: P. Byrne, 1795. St. George Tucker, ViW.

171 Reeves, John. *History of the English law from the time of the Saxons to the end of the reign of Philip and Mary.*

[55]The title of the 1721 edition is *Les Terms de la Ley: or Certaine difficult and obscure Words and Terms of the Common and Statute Laws of this Realm, now in Use, expounded and explained.*

[56]The Yeates library contains two copies of this edition.

[57]Vols. 3 and 4 only.

[58]Vols. 1, 3, and 4 only.

[59]American editions are listed in James, 67.

2nd ed., 4 vols., London: E. Brooke, 1787. John Adams, MB; Benjamin Chew, PPCl; Theophilus Parsons* (22); Jasper Yeates, PLHi.

172 Richardson, Robert. *The Attorney's Practice in the Court of Common Pleas: or, an Introduction to the knowledge of the practice of that court . . . .*
Benet Oldham* (407); John Mercer* (200).

1st ed., London: Henry Lintot, 1741. St. George Tucker, ViW.

2nd ed., enlarged, 2 vols., London: T. Woodward, 1746. James Grindlay* (282); Thomas Jefferson, DLC.

3rd ed., enlarged, 2 vols., London: D. Browne, J. Shuckburgh, T. Osborne, 1758. Jasper Yeates, PLHi.

173 Richardson, Robert. *The Attorney's Practice in the Court of King's Bench . . . .*
James Grindlay* (282); John Mercer* (200); Benet Oldham* (407).

1st ed., London: T. Woodward, 1739. Jasper Yeates, PLHi.

3rd ed., enlarged, 2 vols., London: T. Woodward, 1750. Thomas Jefferson, DLC.

4th ed., enlarged, 2 vols., London: D. Browne, T. Shuckburgh, F. Worratt, 1759. Benjamin Chew, PPCl; Jasper Yeates, PLHi.

174 Robinson, Robert. *The Law of Inheritances in Fee, Laid Down in a New Method . . . .*[60]

[60]The title of the third edition is *A Discourse concerning Inheritances in fee simple . . . .*

2nd ed., London: Ward and Chandler, n.d.[1755].[61] Jasper Yeates, PLHi.

3rd ed., enlarged, London: W. Wyatt, J. Worrall, W. Sandby, 1758. Thomas Jefferson, DLC.

175 *Rules and Orders of the Court of Chancery . . . .*

3rd ed., London; J. Walthoe, 1724. Thomas Jefferson, DLC.

4th ed., enlarged, with notes by F. Hargrave, London: E. & R. Nutt and R. Gosling, 1739. Thomas Jefferson, DLC.

176 Rutherforth, Thomas. *Institutes of Natural Law; being the substance of a Course of Lectures on Grotius de Jure Belli et Pacis.*

1st ed., 2 vols., Cambridge: J. Bentham, 1754–56. John Jay, NNC-L; Theophilus Parsons* (22); Jasper Yeates, PLHi.[62]

3rd ed., 2 vols., London: William Young, 1799. John Adams, MB.

177 Sacheverell, Henry. *The Tryal of Dr. Henry Sacheverell, before the House of Peers, for High Crimes and Misdemeanors; upon an Impeachment . . . .*

London: Jacob Tonson, 1710. Ralph Assheton* (368); William Byrd II* (419); Robert Carter* (149); Benjamin Chew, PPCl;[63] Thomas Jefferson, DLC.

[61]Two London printings occurred in 1755; the other imprint, published by Henry Lintot, bears the title of the third edition.

[62]Vol. 1 only.

[63]There are two copies in the Chew library.

178 Saint-Germain, Christopher. *Doctor and Student: or, Dialogues between a Doctor of Divinity, and a Student in the Laws of England . . . .*
James Grindlay* (282); John Mercer* (200); Benet Oldham* (407); Robert Treat Paine.*

London: R. Gosling, 1721. Benjamin Chew, PPCl; Theophilus Parsons* (19).

16th ed., revised and enlarged, London: J. Worrall, 1761. Jasper Yeates, PLHi.

179 Salmon, Thomas. *A New Abridgment and Critical Review of the State Trials, and impeachments for high-treason . . . .*
John Mercer* (200).

London: J. and J. Hazard, W. Mears, J. Mechell and J. Applebee, C. Ward and R. Chandler, 1738. Thomas Jefferson, DLC.

180 Sampson, Euer. *A System of Pleading, Including a Translation of the Doctrina Placitandi . . . .*

London: William Owen, 1771. Benjamin Chew, PPCl; Jasper Yeates, PLHi.

181 Scroggs, Sir William. *The Practice of Courts-Leet, and Courts-Baron.*
William Smith, Sr.* (185).

3rd ed., enlarged, London: J. Walthoe, 1714. Thomas Jefferson, DLC.

182 Selden, John. *Opera Omnia, Tam Edita Quam Inedita.*

David Wilkins, ed., 3 vols. in 6, London: J. Walthoe, G. Conyers, J. Knapton, 1726. John Adams, MB; James Logan, PPL; Jasper Yeates, PLHi.

183 Sheppard, William. *The Touch-Stone of Common Assurances . . . .*

4th ed., revised and corrected, London: P. Uriel, 1780. Benjamin Chew, PPCl.

6th ed., revised and corrected, Dublin: John Exshaw, 1785. Theophilus Parsons* (22).

184 Spelman, Sir Henry. *The English Works of Sir Henry Spelman, Kt . . . with his posthumous works relating to the laws and antiquities of England.*
William Smith, Sr.* (182).

2nd ed., revised, London: D. Browne, Sr. and Jr., W. Mears, F. Clay, 1723. Jasper Yeates, PLHi.

185 *The Statutes at Large concerning Bankrupts . . . .*
Robert Carter* (147).

With notes by Francis Hargrave, London: 1765. John Mercer* (200).

186 Stubbs, William, and Talmash, G. *The Crown Circuit Companion.*
John Mercer* (200); Robert Treat Paine*; William Smith, Sr.* (189).

1st ed., 3 vols. in 1, London: J. Mechell and J. Bailey, 1738. Joseph Murray, NNC-L.

2nd ed., 2 vols., London: Henry Lintot, 1749. John Jay, NNC-L.

4th ed., Dublin: Sarah Cotter, 1762. Jasper Yeates, PLHi.

4th ed., London: J. Worrell and B. Tovey, 1768. John Adams, MB; Theophilus Parsons* (18).

187 Style, William. *Style's Practical Register, Begun in the Reign of King Charles I.*
James Alexander* (173); William Byrd II* (419); Robert Carter* (261); Francis Dana*; James Grindlay* (282).

4th ed., enlarged, John Lilly, ed., London: C. Harper, D. Brown, J. Walthoe, and D. Midwinter, 1707. John Adams, MB; Thomas Jefferson, DLC.

188 Swinburne, Henry. *A Treatise of Testaments and Last Wills, compiled out of the laws ecclesiastical, civil, and canon . . . .*
Robert Carter* (147); Robert Treat Paine.*

5th ed., corrected and enlarged, London: E. & R. Nutt & R. Gosling, 1728. John Adams, MB; Benjamin Chew*; John Jay, NNC-L; Thomas Jefferson, DLC; William Smith, Sr.* (183).

6th ed., corrected and enlarged, London: Henry Lintot, 1743. Jasper Yeates, PLHi.

189 Taylor, John. *Elements of the Civil Law.*
St. George Tucker* (74).

3rd ed., London: Charles Bathurst, 1769. Thomas Jefferson, DLC.

190 *Tenants Law: or, the Laws Concerning Landlords, Tenants and Farmers . . . .*

13th ed., London: T. Waller, 1750. Thomas Jefferson, DLC.

14th ed., London: S. Richardson and C. Lintot, 1760. St. George Tucker, ViW.

191 Townesend, George. *A Preparative to Pleading. Being a work intended for the instruction and help of young clerks of the Court of Common pleas.*
James Alexander* (174); Robert Carter* (148); William Smith, Sr.* (187); St. George Tucker* (78).

3rd ed., enlarged, London: J. Harrison and W. Mears, 1713. Thomas Jefferson, DLC.

192 *A Treatise of Distresses, Replevins, and Avowries, in the Courts at Westminster, County-Courts, Hundred-Courts, etc. . . .*
Ralph Assheton* (361); John Mercer* (200).

193 *A Treatise of Frauds, Covins, and Collusions . . . all illustrated and explained in several adjudged cases under each proper title, at common law, and in courts of equity.*

London: T. Osborne and S. Butler, 1710. James Alexander* (174); Ralph Assheton* (366); Thomas Jefferson, DLC.

194 Tremaine, Sir John. *Placita Coronae: or, Pleas of the Crown in Matters Criminal and Civil.*
William Smith, Sr.* (184).

Revised ed., John Rice, London: T. Ward, T. Wooton, and E. Valentine, 1723. Benjamin Chew, PPCl; Thomas Jefferson, DLC; Jasper Yeates, PLHi.
2 vols., Dublin: 1795. Theophilus Parsons* (23).

195 Tyrrell, James. *A Brief Disquisition of the Law of Nature, according to the principles and method laid down in the Reverend Dr. Cumberland's . . . Latin treatise on that subject.*
James Grindlay* (282); William Smith, Sr.* (186).

196 de Vattel, Emmerich. *The Law of Nations: or Principles of the law of Nature applied to the conduct and affairs of nations and sovereigns.*[64]
Francis Dana*; Robert Treat Paine.*

2 vols. in 1, London: J. Newberry, J. Richardson, T. Carton, J. Longmans, P. Law, J. Fuller, J. Csote, G. Kearsley, 1759. John Jay, NNC-L; St. George Tucker* (72).

New, corrected ed., London: G.C.J. and J. Robinson; Whieldon & Butterworth, 1793. Jasper Yeates, PLHi.

197 Vidian, Andrew. *The Exact Pleader: A Book of Entries of Choice, Select and Special Pleadings in the Court of King's Bench . . . .*
William Smith, Sr.* (184).

London: Christopher Wilkinson, Tho. Dring, and Charles Harper, 1784. Jasper Yeates, PLHi.

198 Viner, Charles. *A General Abridgment of Law and Equity, alphabetically digested under proper titles . . . .*

1st ed., 24 vols., Aldershot: Charles Viner, 1742–53. John Adams, MB;[65] Benjamin Chew, PPCl;[66] John Jay, NNC-L;[67] Thomas Jefferson, DLC;[68] John Mercer* (200); Peter Leigh* (257); Joseph Murray, NNC-L;[69] Jasper Yeates, PLHi.[70]

[64]Thomas Jefferson's French edition of 1775 is in DLC. For American editions see James, 116.
[65]Vols. 1–23 only.
[66]Vols. 1–8 only.
[67]Vols. 1–23 only.
[68]Vols. 1–9 only.
[69]Vols. 10, 20 only.
[70]Vols. 1–22, plus index vol.

2nd ed., 24 vols., London: G.G.J. and J. Robinson, 1791–94. Theophilus Parsons* (23).

199 Ward, Robert Plumer. *An Enquiry into the Foundation and History of the Law of Nations in Europe, from the time of the Greeks and Romans to the age of Grotius.*

2 vols., Dublin: P. Wogan, P. Byrne, W. Jones, and J. Rice, 1795. Thomas Jefferson, DLC.

2 vols., London: J. Butterworth, 1795. Theophilus Parsons* (23); Jasper Yeates, PLHi.

200 Washington, Joseph. *An Exact Abridgment of all the Statutes of King William and Queen Mary, and of King William III. in force and use.*
James Alexander* (173); William Byrd II* (418); James Grindlay* (282).

2 vols., London: Her Majesty's Printers and the assigns of R. and E. Atkyns, 1708. Thomas Jefferson, DLC.

201 Watson, William. *The Clergy-Man's Law: or, the Compleat Incumbent . . . .*

4th ed., revised and enlarged, London: D. Midwinter, W. Innys, T. Woodward, 1747. Thomas Jefferson, DLC; Jasper Yeates, PLHi.

202 Wentworth, Thomas. *The Office and Duty of Executors: or, A treatise directing testators to form, and executors to perform their wills and testaments according to law.*
James Grindlay* (281); William Smith, Sr.* (186).

Henry Curson, ed., London: J. Place, 1703. John Mercer* (201).

Henry Curson, ed., London: D. Browne, 1720. Theophilus Parsons* (23).

203 Weskett, John. *A Complete Digest of the Theory, Laws, and Practice of Insurance.*

1st ed., London: Frys, Couchman & Collier, 1781. Theophilus Parsons* (23); Jasper Yeates, PLHi.

204 Wingate, Edmund. *An Exact Abridgment of all the Statutes in Force and Use from the beginning of Magna charta.* James Alexander* (173); William Byrd II* (418); Robert Carter* (148); James Grindlay* (282).

10th ed., revised and enlarged, London: Her Majesty's Printers and the assigns of R. Atkins and E. Atkins, 1704. Thomas Jefferson, DLC.

205 von Wolff, Christian, Baron. *Institutions du Droit de la Nature et des Gens . . . .*

1st ed., 6 vols., Leiden: E. Luzac, 1772. John Adams, MB; Thomas Jefferson, DLC.

206 Wood, Edward. *A Complete body of Conveyancing, in Theory and Practice . . . .* Robert Treat Paine.*

4th ed., 3 vols., London: His Majesty's Law Printers, 1777. Theophilus Parsons* (23).

5th ed., revised, corrected, and enlarged, John J. Powell, ed., 3 vols., London: J. Johnson, 1790–93. Jasper Yeates, PLHi.

207 Wood, Thomas. *An Institute of the Laws of England; or, The Laws of England in their Natural Order, according to Common Use.*

Francis Dana*; James Grindlay* (280, 281); John Mercer* (200); Benet Oldham* (407).

1st ed., 4 vols. in 2, London: Richard Sare, 1720. James Logan, PPL.

2nd ed., corrected and enlarged, London: Richard Sare, 1722. Ralph Assheton* (361).

5th ed., enlarged, London: Bernard Lintot and Richard Williamson, 1734. Theophilus Parsons* (23).

6th ed., London: Henry Lintot and Thomas Osborne, 1738. Jasper Yeates, PLHi.

208 Wood, Thomas. *A New Institute of the Imperial, or Civil Law.*
James Grindlay* (280).

3rd ed., corrected, 2 parts in 1 vol., London: Richard Sare, 1721. James Logan, PPL.

4th ed., corrected, London: J. and J. Knapton, D. Midwinter & A. Ward, 1730. Jasper Yeates, PLHi.

209 Woodeson, Richard. *A Systematic View of the Laws of England; as treated of in a course of Vinerian lectures, read at Oxford, during a series of years, commencing in Michaelmas term, 1777.*

3 vols., Dublin: E. Lynch, P. Wogan, P. Byrne, 1792–94. Thomas Jefferson, DLC. Theophilus Parsons* (23); Jasper Yeates, PLHi.[71]

3 vols., London: Thomas Payne, 1792. Jasper Yeates, PLHi.[72]

[71]Vol. 3 only.
[72]Vols. 1, 2 only.

210 Worrall, John. *Bibliotheca Legum: or, A New and Compleat List of the Common and Statute Law Books of this Realm . . . .*
Robert Treat Paine.*

4th ed., enlarged, London: J. Worrall, 1738. James Logan, PPL.

New ed., corrected, revised, and enlarged, London: Edward Brooke, 1776. St. George Tucker, ViW; Jasper Yeates, PLHi.

New ed., corrected and revised, London: Edward Brooke, 1788.[73] Jasper Yeates, PLHi.

211 Wright, Sir Martin. *Introduction to the Law of Tenures . . . .*
Peter Leigh* (257).

2nd ed., London: 1730. Theophilus Parsons* (23).

3rd ed., London: J. Nourse, 1768. Jasper Yeates, PLHi.

3rd ed., Dublin: James Moore, 1792. St. George Tucker, ViW.

212 Yorke, Charles. *Some Considerations on the Law of Forfeitures for High Treason . . . .*

4th ed., corrected and enlarged, London: J. Williams, 1775. Jasper Yeates, PLHi.

4th ed., corrected and enlarged, Edinburgh: John Donaldson, 1778. Theophilus Parsons* (23); St. George Tucker, ViW.

[73]The title of this edition is *Bibliotheca Legum Angliae, Part I. Or, a Catalogue of the Common and Statute Law Books of this Realm . . . .* The second part by Edward Brooke, published in a second volume, is entitled *Bibliotheca Legum Angliae, Part II. Containing a General Account of the Laws and Law-Writers of England.* A copy of the 1788 edition, published by Brooke in London, is in the library of Jasper Yeates, PLHi.

Appendix A
TITLES BY CATEGORY AND FREQUENCY OF USE

ABRIDGMENTS

General — *Number of Holdings*

- D'Anvers, *A General Abridgment* 13
- Bacon, *A New Abridgment* 10
- Viner, *A General Abridgment* 9
- Lilly, *The Practical Register* 8
- Comyns, *A Digest of the Laws* 4
- Finch, *Law, or a Discourse Thereof* 4
- Jacob, *Common Law Common-placed* 2
- Jacob, *Every Man His Own Lawyer* 2
- Jacob, *Law Grammar* 2
- *The Laws of England Delineated* 2
- Lilly, *A Continuation of the Practical Register* 2

Statutes — *Number of Holdings*

- Wingate, *An Exact Abridgment* 5
- Jacob, *Statute-Law Common-Plac'd* 5
- Washington, *An Exact Abridgment* 4
- Barrington, *Observations* 3
- *Readings upon the Statute Law* 3

Cases

- Nelson, *An Abridgment of the Common Law* 7
- *A General Abridgment of Cases in Equity* 6
- *A New Abridgment of . . . State Trials* 2
- *Precedents in Chancery* 2

COMMENTARIES AND INSTITUTES

- Blackstone, *Commentaries* 10
- Wood, *Institutes of the Laws of England* 8
- Saint-Germain, *Doctor and Student* 7
- Hale, *History of the Common Law* 6
- Blackstone, *Law Tracts* 4
- Woodeson, *A Systematic View of the Laws* 4
- Blackstone, *Analysis of the Laws* 3
- Plowden, *Commentaries or Reports* 3

PRACTICE MANUALS

General

Title	Count
Bohun, *Institutio Legalis*	6
Brown, *Modus Intrandi*	5
Covert, *Scrivener's Guide*	5
Gardiner, *A Doctrine of Demurrers*	4
Sampson, *A System of Pleading*	2

Common Law Courts

Title	Count
Lilly, *Modern Entries*	10
Officium Clerici Pacis	9
Richardson, *Attorney's Practice in King's Bench*	7
Brown, *A . . . Treatise of Fines*	6
Clift, *A New Book of Declarations*	6
Richardson, *Attorney's Practice in Common Pleas*	6
Booth, *Nature and Practice of Real Actions*	5
Gardiner, *Instructor Clericalis, Part III*	5
Gardiner, *Instructor Clericalis, Part V*	5
Levinz, *A Collection of . . . Modern Entries*	5
Townesend, *Preparative to Pleading*	5
Barnes, *Notes of Cases*	4
Gardiner, *Instructor Clericalis, Part I*	4
Gardiner, *Instructor Clericalis, Part IV*	4
Impey, *New Instructor Clericalis*	4
Mallory, *Attorney's Pocket Companion*	4
Bohun, *Declarations and Pleadings*	3
Mallory, *Modern Entries*	3
Bowman, *English Pleader*	2
Clerk's Manual	2
Compleat Clerk in Court	2
Cornwall, *Tables to the Modern Printed Precedents*	2
Crompton, *Practice Common-placed*	2
Gardiner, *Instructor Clericalis, Part II*	2
Gardiner, *Practick Part of the Law*	2
Heath, *Maxims and Rules of Pleading*	2
Morgan, *Attorney's Vade Mecum*	2
Pleader's Assistant	2
Vidian, *Exact Pleader*	2

Chancery

Title	Count
Bohun, *Cursus cancellariae*	6
Brown, *Praxis Almae Curiae Cancellariae*	6
Brown, *Clerk's Tutor in Chancery*	4
Harrison, *Accomplish'd Practiser*	4
Practical Register in Chancery	4
Redesdale, *Treatise on Pleading*	4
Clerk's Manual	2
Hinde, *Modern Practice*	2

Admiralty

Title	Count
Clerke, *Practice of the Court of Admiralty*	2

Ecclesiastical Courts

Conset, *Practice of Spiritual Courts*	3
Cockburn, *Clerk's Assistant*	2
Floyer, *Proctor's Practice*	2
Mallory, *Quare Impedit*	2

CONVEYANCING MANUALS

Bridgman, *Bridgman's Conveyances*	5
Lilly, *Practical Conveyancer*	5
Horsman, *Precedents*	3
Modern Conveyancer	3
Wood, *Complete Body of Conveyancing*	3
Pigott, *New Precedents*	2
Pocket Conveyancer	2

LAW DICTIONARIES

Jacob, *A New Law-Dictionary*	12
Cowell, *Law Dictionary, or the Interpreter*	6
The Law-French Dictionary	6
Rastell, *Termes de la Ley*	4
Blount, *Law-Dictionary and Glossary*	3
Cunningham, *New and Complete Law-Dictionary*	3

FORMULARIES

Fitzherbert, *New Natura Brevium*	13
Officium Clerici Pacis	9
Bohun, *English Lawyer*	2
Book of Oaths	2

JUSTICE OF THE PEACE MANUALS

Officium Clerici Pacis	9
Burn, *Justice of the Peace*	6
Dalton, *Country Justice*	4
Nelson, *Office and Authority*	3
Blackerby, *Cases in Law*	2
Kilburne, *Choice Presidents*	2

LEGAL BIBLIOGRAPHY

Worrall, *Bibliotheca Legum*	5
Bassett, *Catalogue*	2

TREATISES

Admiralty

Molloy, *De Jure Maritimo et Navali* 12
Justice, *A General Treatise* 4

Civil Law and Roman Law

Domat, *The Civil Law* 6
Digesti Justiniani Institutionum 3
Wood, *New Institute of . . . Civil Law* 3
Noodt, *Opera Omnia Juridica* 2
Taylor, *Elements of Civil Law* 2

Constitutional Law

de Lolme, *The Constitution of England* 4
Care, *English Liberties* 3
Hargrave, *A Collection of Tracts* 3
Kames, *Essays* 3
Hargrave, *Collecteana Juridica* 2

Courts, Procedure, and Evidence

Duncombe, *Tryals per pais* 8
Buller, *Introduction to Trials at Nisi Prius* 7
Gilbert, *The Law of Evidence* 6
Dalton, *Officium Vicecomitum* 5
The Compleat Sheriff 4
Gardiner, *The Doctrine of Demurrers* 4
Greenwood, *The Authority of County Courts* 4
The Law of Errors 4
Nelson, *The Law of Evidence* 4
The Law of Executions 3
Foley, *Laws Relating to the Poor* 2
Highmore, *A Digest of . . . Bail* 2
Rules and Orders of the Court of Chancery 2
Scroggs, *The Practice of Courts-Leet* 2

Criminal Law

Hale, *Historia Placitorum Coronae* 11
Hawkins, *A Treatise of . . . Pleas of the Crown* 11
Stubbs, *Crown Circuit Companion* 8
Foster, *Report . . . and Some Discourses* 5
The Tryal of Dr. Henry Sacheverell 5
Tremaine, *Placita Coronae* 5
Hale, *Pleas of the Crown* 4
Yorke, *Some Considerations on . . . Forfeitures* 3
The Tryal of Thomas Earl of Macclesfield 2
Salmon, *New Abridgment of . . . State Trials* 2

Customary and Local Law

The Law of Corporations 4
Bohun, *Privilegia Londini* 2
The Law of Commons and Commoners 2
Scroggs, *The Practice of Courts-Leet* 2

Ecclesiastical Law (General)

Burn, *Ecclesiastical Law* 4
Conset, *The Practice of Spiritual Courts* 3

Gibson, *Codex Juris Ecclesiastici Anglicani* 2
Mallory, *Quare Impedit* 2
Watson, *Clergy-man's Law* 2

Ecclesiastical Law (Decedent Estates)

Nelson, *Lex Testamentaria* 10
Swinburne, *A Treatise of Testaments* 8
Godolphin, *Orphan's Legacy* 6
The Law of Executors and Administrators 4
Wentworth, *Office and Duties of Executors* 4
Kames, *Essays* 3
Powell, *Essay upon . . . Devises* 3
Gilbert, *The Law of Devises* 2
Hale, *De Successionibus apud Anglos* 2
Of Last Wills and Testaments 2

Equity

Francis, *Maxims of Equity* 4
Kames, *Principles of Equity* 4
Ballow, *A Treatise of Equity* 3
A Treatise of Frauds, Covins and Collusions 3

Family Law

Baron and Feme 5
Infant's Lawyer 3

Insurance

Park, *Marine Insurance* 3
Miller, *Elements of Insurance* 2
Weskett, *Digest of Insurance* 2

International Law

Grotius, *Of the Rights of War and Peace* 5
de Vattel, *The Law of Nations* 5
Grotius, *De Jure Belli et Pacis* 3
Ward, *Enquiry into . . . the Law of Nations* 2

Law Merchant

Molloy, *De Jure Maritimo et Navali* 12
Jacob, *Lex Mercatoria* 7
Beawes, *Lex Mercatoria Rediviva* 6
A General Treatise of Naval Trade 6
Cunningham, *The Law of Bills of Exchange* 5
Kyd, *A Treatise on . . . Bills of Exchange* 4
Bacon, *The Compleat Arbitrator* 2
Cooke, *Compendious System of . . . Bankrupt Laws* 2
Goodinge, *The Law Against Bankrupts* 2
The Statutes . . . Concerning Bankrupts 2

Legal History

Saint-Germain, *Doctor and Student* 7
Fortescue, *De Laudibus Legum Angliae* 6
Hale, *History of the Common Law* 6
Gilbert, *History and Practice . . . of Common Pleas* 4
Reeves, *History of English Law* 4
Goguet, *The Origin of Laws* 3
Kames, *Essays . . . Concerning British Antiquities* 3
Kames, *Historical Law-Tracts* 3
Selden, *Opera Omnia* 3
Burroughs, *The History of Chancery* 2

Horne, *Mirrour of Justices* 2
Spelman, *English Works* 2
Ward, *An Enquiry into the History of the Law* 2

Natural Law

von Pufendorf, *Law of Nature and Nations* 9
Rutherforth, *Institutes of Natural Law* 4
Cumberland, *A Treatise of the Laws of Nature* 3
von Pufendorf, *De Officio Hominis* 3
Heineccius, *Methodical System of Universal Law* 2
von Pufendorf, *Le Droit de la Nature et des Gens* 2
Tyrell, *Brief Disquisition* 2
von Wolff, *Institutions du Droit de la Nature* 2

Personal Property

The Law of Covenants 5
Powell, *Essay upon . . . Contracts* 5
Gilbert, *Law of Distresses and Replevins* 4
Gilbert, *Law of Uses and Trusts* 2
Jones, *Essay upon . . . Bailments* 2
Powell, *Essay on . . . Powers* 2
A Treatise of Distresses, Replevins and Avowries 2

Real Property

Coke, . . . *A Commentary upon Littleton* 13
The Law of Ejectments 10
Booth, *Nature and Practice of Real Actions* 5
Carter, *Lex Vadiorum* 5
Fearne, *Essay on . . . Contingent Remainders* 5
Gilbert, *A Treatise of Tenures* 5
Brown, *Compendious . . . Treatise of Fines* 4
Gilbert, *Law of Distresses and Replevins* 4
Hawkins, *Abridgment of the first part of Coke's Institutes* 4
Wright, *Introduction to the Law of Tenures* 2
Curson, *Law Concerning Estates Taile* 2
Gilbert, *Law of Uses and Trusts* 2
The Law of Commons and Commoners 2
Pigott, *A Treatise of Common Recoveries* 2
Powell, *Essay on . . . Powers* 2
Powell, *Treatise upon . . . Mortgages* 2
Sheppard, *Touch-stone of Common Assurances* 2
Robinson, *Law of Inheritance in Fee* 2
Tenant's Law 2

Torts

Carter, *A Treatise Concerning Trespasses* 4
The Law of Actions on the Case 2

Appendix B
LAW LIBRARY LISTS

Although a number of lists used in this book have not been published previously, it is appropriate that they appear in an appendix to the main work. Where law books on the lists have been segregated from other titles in a given library, we have printed only the legal section of the list. On the other hand if the library is classified either by the size of the volumes or by some other system not related to the subject of the books, all titles are included in the list as printed.

The format and text of the original manuscript have been followed as closely as possible. Superscript letters have been brought to line, and expansions have been inserted in brackets only when the lowering of the letter caused confusion in meaning. Tears or obliterations have been shown by square brackets, with a footnote to show the flaw in the original document. Monetary evaluations have been shown in the printed text as they appear in the manuscript; however columnar amounts have been rendered to show pounds, shillings, and pence separated by colons. Peculiar and phonetic spellings have been retained from the original manuscript, but when clarification is required, it is supplied in a footnote.

Omitted from this appendix is the library list of Robert Treat Paine, soon to be published in an edition of Paine's letters and papers being prepared under the direction of Stephen T. Riley of the Massachusetts Historical Society. The compiler is grateful to the Bucks County Historical Society and the Massachusetts Historical Society for their gracious permission to publish the John Mercer and Francis Dana lists. He acknowledges with thanks the kindness of the staff of the South Carolina Department of Archives and History in making available the lists of James Grindlay, Peter Leigh, and Benet Oldham.

FRANCIS DANA[1]

Year Books 7 Vol Folio
Plowdens Reports 1 Vol.
Jacob's Dictionary
Bible Folio
Fortescue 1 V.
Hobarts Reports 2 V.
Wood's Institutes 1 V.
Coke on Littleton 1 V.
Hawkin's Pleas of the Crown 1 V.
Lilly's Practical Register 1 V.
Do Practical Conveyancer
Lilly's Entries 1 V.
Clift's Do. 1 V.
Levinz's Entries 2 V.
Liber Placitam 1 V.
Lent to Mr. Ellery
Thesaurus Brevium 1 V.
Compleat Clerk & Scrivner's Guide 2 V.
Coke's Reports 7 V. 4o
Rolle's Abridgment 2 V.
Do.Reports 2 V.
Burrows Reports 3 V.
Willsons Reports 1 V.
Modern Reports 2 V.
Saunder's Reports 2 V.
Cases of Equity 1 V.
Fitzgibbon's Reports 1 V.
Dalton's Justice 1 V.
Modern Cases 1 V.
Dalton's Sheriffs 1 V.
Ainsworth's Dictionary 1 V.
Taylor on Orig. Sin 1 V.
Diseases of Wom: wth Child 1 V.
Preceptor 2 V.
Bailey's Dictionary 1 V.
Sr. Fr. Bacon's Essays 1 V.
Present for an Apprentice 1 V.
Blackstone 4 V.
Natura Brevium 1 V.
Burrow's Decisions 1 V.
Gravesande's Exp. 2 V.
Vattel Law of N. 1 V.
Locke's Works 4 V.
Locke's Essays 2 V.

[1]Dana Papers, Massachusetts Historical Society, Boston, Mass. This is the most complete list of books in the Dana Papers, the others appearing to be notations concerning books borrowed. The document is headed, "A List of the Books of Francis Dana Esqr/ Having his Coat of Arms."

Watt's Logic 1 V.
Ward's Mathem. 1 V.
Homer's Illius 1 V.
Horace 1 V.
Terence 1 V.
Euclid's Elements 1 V.
Watts's Astronomy 1 V.
Love's Art of Surveyg 1 V.
Hammond's Algebra 1 V.
Virgil 1 V.
Burn's Justice 3 Vol.
Molloy's de Jure Maritimo 1 V. Sea Laws
Hume's Essays 2 Vol.
Do. History of Eng. 8 V.
Voltair Europe 3 V.
Robertson's History of Ch. 5 3 V.
Voltair Philosophical Dic. 1 V.
Crimes & Punishments 1 V.
Exam. of Edwards's Freedom of the Will 1 V.
French Grammer
Homer's Iliad Greek 1 V.
Salmon's Gazetteer 1 V.
Milton's Paradise lost 1 V.
Cicero de Officiis 1 V.
Instructor Clericalis 7 Vol.
Trials par Pais 1 V.
Jus Imperii N. Servitutis 1 V.
Settlements & Removals 1 V.
Nelson's Justice 1 V.
Kilburne's Do. 1 V.
Lex Testamentaria 1 V.
Spectator 9 V.
History of Eng in Letters 2 V.
Freeholder 1 V.
Fordyce Sermons 1 V.
Yorick's Do. 2 V.
Do. Sentimental Jour. 1 V.
Lambard's Eirenarcha 1 V.
Judgments 1 V.
Officium Clerici Pacis 1 V.
Pope's Homer 4 V.
Pope's Works 17 V.
Young's Works 4 V.
Vade Mecum 1 V.
Style's Practical Regr 1 V. Lent to Mr. Ellery
Regula placitandi 1 V. Lent to Same
Statutes relating to High Treason 1 Vol.
Leonard's Reports 2 Vol.

JAMES GRINDLAY[2]

Library of Books to wit Folios

Horsemans Conveyancer 3 Vols 15: :
Saunders Reports 2 Vols 8: :

[2]Inventories 1763–67, pp. 280–84, South Carolina Department of Archives and History, Columbia, S.C. The values are in South Carolina currency, which was one-seventh the value of sterling money.

Lord Raymonds Reports 2 Vols 20: :
Stranges Reports 2 Vols 15: :
Barnardistons Reports in Kings Bench 5: :
Ditto Reports in Chancery 5: :
Comyns Reports 5: :
Hales Pleas of the Crown 2 Vols 6: :
An Institute of the law of Scotland 3 Vols 10: :
Salkelds Reports 3 Vols £ 7 Comberbachs Reports £ 3 10: :
Farresleys Reports 20/ Crokes Reports 3 parts £ 20 21: :
Modern Reports 6 Vols. £ 12 Cases in Chancery £ 5 17: :
Cases in Equity abridged 4: :
Woods Institutes of the Civil Law 3: :
Lillys Abridgement 2 Vols 7: :
Carthews Reports £ 4 Ventris's Reports £4 8: :
Precedents in Conveyancing 4: :
Freemans Pleas of the Crown 3: :
Modern Entries 2 Vols £ 5 Clifts Entries £ 3 8: :
Fitzgibbons Reports £ 3 3: :
Hawkins Pleas of the Crown 2 Vols 6: :
Danvers Abridgement 3 Vols 6: :
Peere Williams Reports 3 Vols 25: :
Vernons Cases in Chancery 2 Vols 12: :
Reports in Chancery £5 Cases in Law & Equity £ 3 8: :
Reports in Equity £ 3 Modern Cases in Equity £ 4 7: :
Talbots Cases £ 3 Nelsons Chancery Reports £ 3 6: :
Reports in Chancery & Kings Bench 2: :
Levings Reports 3 parts 9: :
Swinburn's Treatice of Wills 4: :
Bulstrodes Reports 4: :
Trots Laws of South Carolina with Sundry Loose Parcels 20: :
Do in Manuscript 20/ Jacobs Law Dictionary £ 5 6: :

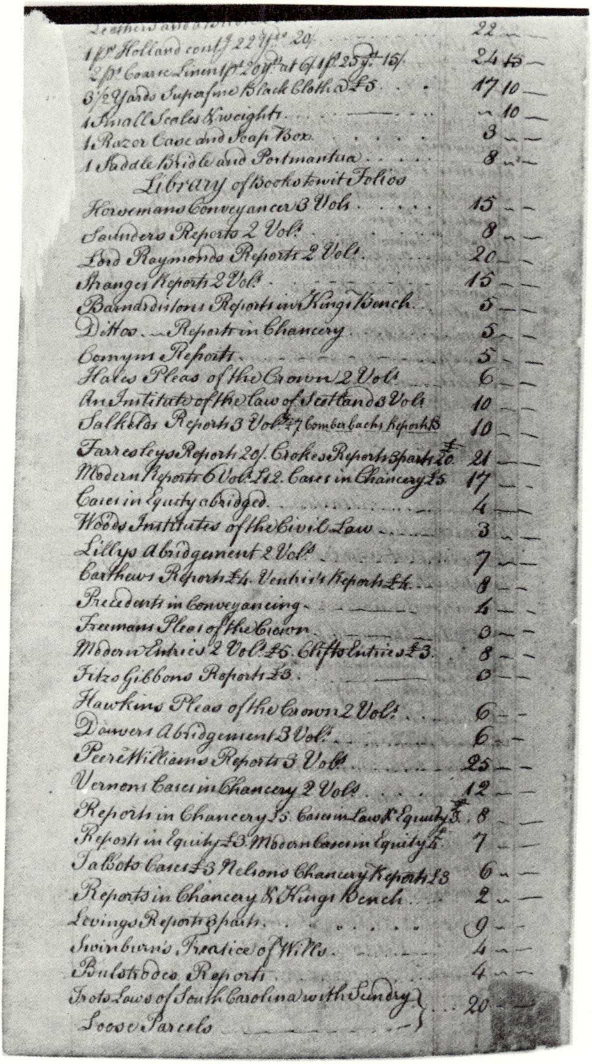

	£	s	d
[illegible]	22	—	—
1 p^r Holland cont^g 22 y^ds 20/	24	15	—
2 p^s Coarse Linen 1 p^s 20 y^ds at 6/ 1 p^s 25 y^ds 15/			
3½ Yards Superfine Black Cloth @ £5	17	10	—
1 Small Scales & weights	—	10	—
1 Razor Case and Soap Box	3	—	—
1 Saddle Bridle and Portmantua	8	—	—
Library of Books to wit Folios			
Horsemans Conveyancer 3 Vols	15	—	—
Saunders Reports 2 Vol^s	8	—	—
Lord Raymonds Reports 2 Vol^s	20	—	—
Stranges Reports 2 Vol^s	15	—	—
Barnardistons Reports in Kings Bench	5	—	—
Dittos — Report in Chancery	5	—	—
Comyns Reports	5	—	—
Hales Pleas of the Crown 2 Vol^s	6	—	—
An Institute of the Law of Scotland 3 Vols	10	—	—
Salkelds Reports 3 Vol^s £7 Comberbachs Reports £3	10	—	—
Farresleys Reports 20/. Crokes Reports 3 parts £20.	21	—	—
Modern Reports 6 Vol^s £12. Cases in Chancery £5	17	—	—
Cases in Equity abridged	4	—	—
Woods Institutes of the Civil Law	3	—	—
Lillys Abridgement 2 Vol^s	7	—	—
Carthews Reports £4. Ventris's Reports £4	8	—	—
Precedents in Conveyancing	4	—	—
Freemans Pleas of the Crown	3	—	—
Modern Entries 2 Vol^s £5. Cliftons Entries £3	8	—	—
Fitzo Gibbons Reports £3	3	—	—
Hawkins Pleas of the Crown 2 Vol^s	6	—	—
Danvers Abridgement 3 Vol^s	6	—	—
Peere Williams Reports 3 Vol^s	25	—	—
Vernons Cases in Chancery 2 Vol^s	12	—	—
Reports in Chancery £5. Cases in Law & Equity £3	8	—	—
Reports in Equity £3. Modern Cases in Equity £4	7	—	—
Talbots Cases £3 Nelsons Chancery Reports £3	6	—	—
Reports in Chancery & Kings Bench	2	—	—
Levings Reports 3 parts	9	—	—
Swinburn's Treatice of Wills	4	—	—
Bulstrodes Reports	4	—	—
Trots Laws of South Carolina with Sundry Loose Parcels	20	—	—

Estate Inventory of Library of James Grindlay.
South Carolina Department of Archives and History, Columbia.

Title	Price
Cock on Lyttleton 60/ Lutwyches Reports 2 Vols £ 15	18: :
Bacons Abridgement 4 Vols	25: :
Rolls Abridgement 2 Vols	7: :
Nelsons Abridgement 3 Vols	6: :
Plowden's Commentaries	3: :
Puffendorfs Law of Nature & Nations	3: :
Let Mercatoria Rediviva	7: :
Reports & Cases of Practice in the Court of Common Pleas	3: :
Palmers Reports £ 3 Styles Reports 40/	5: :
Hobarts Reports 40/ Acts of Parliament 20/	3: :
Lillyes Entries 40/ The Laws of Virginia 20/	3: :
Domates Civil Law 2d Volums	2: :
Woods Institutes £ 5 Lex Mercatoria MayLyn 40/	7: :
A Collection of all the Statutes now in use by Ferdinand Pulton	5: :
Thesaurus Brevium	1:10:
Cok's Institutes 3 & 4 parts	3: :
Liber Placitandi	1:10:
Laws of Jamaica	:10:
Reports of Cases in the Reign of King Charles 2nd	2: :
Townsends Tables 1st Vol	1: :
Savilles Reports	1: :
Acts of Parliament Anno Duodecimo Regni Caroli 2d Regis	1: :
Acts of Do Anno Octavo Regni Gulielmi 3d Regis	1: :
Acts of Do Anno Nono Regni Guglielmi 3d Regis	[1:] :
Crokes Reports 5/ Bridgmans Conveyancer 20/	1: 5:
Salmons Critical Review	5: :
Chambers Dictionary Two Volums	20: :
Josephus Works Two Volumes	7: :
Locks Essay on Human Understanding	2: :
A Collection of Songs and Dialogues	1: :
A Short View of the late Troubles in England	1: :
Origines Sacri by Stillingfleet	3: :

Conspiracies of Pretended Saints : 5:
The Primitive Origination of Mankind 1: :

Quartos

Brownlowes Entries 5/ Placita Latin Rediviva 5/ :10:
Simpsons Justice 50/ Extracts from Marine Treaties 40/ 4:10:
Viners Institutes 40/ Stanford Pleas of the Crown 5/ 2: 5:
Conductor Generalis or Hales Justice 1: :
Montague of Tythes 10/ Sheppards Abridgement 2 Vols 40/ 2:10:
The Office of Executors 5/ A Family Bible £ 5 5: 5:
Smollets History of England 4 Vols 16: :
Christian Dictionary 1: :
Bacons Works abridged 3 Vols 12: :
Littletons Latin Dictionary 2: :
Doddridges Family Expositor 6 Vols 20: :
Crudens Concordance 5: :
Kennetts Parochial Antiquities 3: :
An Indian Bible 5/ Exposition on the Book of Job 2/6 : 7: 6
Doddridges Paraphrase 3 Vols 10: :
Comedy called Andrea 5/ Practical Navigation 10/ :15:

Octavos et Infra

Cockes Reports 7 Vols £20 Gilberts Law of Devices 20/ 21: :
[Co]nsets Practice of Ecclesiastical Courts :10:
[Th]e[3] Compleat Attorney and Solicitor 1: :
A Treatise of Maritime Affairs 2: :
The Law of Errors 10/ The Spirit of Laws 2 Vols £ 4 4:10:
Washingtons Abridgement 2 Vols 2: :
Grays System 20/ Institutes Legalis 20/ 2: :
The Law of Ejectments 10/ Praxis Almae Curiae 2 Vols 2 £ 2:10:
Parliament Debates 9 Vols 13:10:
Naval Trade 2 Vols 3: :

[3]Obliterated by discoloration of the paper.

Title	Price
Barnes Notes in Common Pleas 2 Vols	3:10:
Harrisons practice in Chancery 2 Vols	4: :
The Attorneys practice in the King's Bench 2 Vols	4: :
The Attorneys Practice in the Common Pleas 2 Vols	4: :
The Law of Evidence	1: :
The Modern Practice of the Court of Exchequer	:10:
Cursus Cancillariae 20/ The Law of Trover 15/	1:15:
The Clerks Instructor in the Ecclesiastical Courts	1: :
Styles Practical Register	1: :
Officium Clerici Pacis 5/ The Statute Law commonplaced 10/	:15:
The Scriveners Guid 20/ The law of appeals 10/	1:10:
Blackeleys Cases in Law 10/ The law of Corporations 10/	1: :
Law Quibbles 10/ The Practical Register in Chancery 10/	1: :
The English Pleader 20/ The law of Evidence 5/	1: 5:
Greenwoods on Courts 5/ The law of Ejectments 20/	1: 5:
Clerks Tutor in Chancery 10/ Floyers Proctors Practice 20/	1:10:
The Clerks Remembrancer 10/	:10:
The Modern Conveyancer 2 Vols	1:10:
Two Tracts on Tyths 5/ The Conveyancers Guide 10/	:15:
An Abridgement of all the Statutes 8 Vols	12: :
Readings upon the Statute Law 5 Vols	7: :
The principles of Politic Law 2 Vols	3: :
Nelsons Lex Testamentaria	1:10:
Whitlock's Essays 5/ Wingates Abridgement 60/	3: 5:
The Clerks Instructor in the Kings Bench & Common Pleas	:10:
Johnston Cannons 1st Volume	:10:
An Abstract of Penal Laws	:15:
The Lawyers Logick 10/ The Attorneys Accademy 10/	1: :

Tryals pr Pais 10/ An Exact Abridgment of all the Statutes 10/ 1: :
Ars Clericalis 2 Vols 1: :
Modus Instrandi Placita Generalis : 5:
Kennett of Impropriationis :10:
Clerks Manual 5/ Spelman of Tythes 2/6 : 7:
Tyrells Law of Nature :10:
Hawkins Abridgement of the Institutes : 5:
Browns Entring Clark : 5:
The first part of Cokes Institutes abridged : 5:
Fitzherberts Natura Brevium : 5:
The Excellency of the Law : 5:
Book of Oaths 10/ The Young Clerks Guide 5/ :15:
Acts of Parliament 21 Vols 31: :
Directions for the study of the Law : 2: 6
A Catalogue of Law Books : 2: 6
Jurisdiction or the lawful Authority of Courts : 5:
The whole Office of the Country Justice of Peace : 2: 6
A Compendium of Law 2/6 Law concerng Travellg : 7: 6
Law against Bankrupts 10/ Blounts Tenures 5/ :15:
The Compleat Justice 5/ The Law of Bastardy 2/6 : 7: 6
The Attorneys Pocket Companion : 5:
A Treatise of Hereditary Descents : 5:
The Practical Court of Admiralty : 2: 6
Judge Jenkins Works 2/6 Doctor & student 2/6 : 5:
Carys Reports 2/6 Acts of Parliament 2 Vols 2/6 : 5:
An Abridgement of the Acts of Parliament : 2: 6
The Parsons Guide or the law of Tythes : 2: 6
Parks Curiae Admiralitatis Anglia : 2: 6
A Colection of Remarkable Tryals : 2: 6
Bibliotheque Ancienne & Moderne 3 Vols : 5:
Herveys Dialogues 40/ Watts Logick 20/ 3: :
An Essay on Civil Powers 10/ Andersons Masonry 30/ 2: :
Confession of Faith 1: :

The Parsons Counsellor 5/ Onavia or sin of self Polution 10/ :15:
Fosters Sermons 2 Vols 40/ Bladens Caesar 20/ 3: :
An Examination of Doctr Burnetts Theory of the Earth 1: :
Observations on the History of the Resurrection of Christ 1: :
Fleetwoods Chronicom Preciosum 1: :
Boyers French Dictionary 3:10:
Loves Surveying 15/ Wilsons Surveying 20/ 1:15:
History of the 5 Indian Nations 1:10:
Russels Oeconomy of Nature 1: :
Cambrays Eloquence 1: :
Shaftsburys Characteristicks 3 Vols 5: :
Privilegia Londini 10/ Cardinal Richlieus Letters 20/ 1:10:
Evidences of Religion 10/ The Rule & Exercises of holy Living 10/ 1: :
Bacons Moral Essays :15:
Magazines from the year 1733 to the year 1760 and 3 years loose 28: :
An English Dictionary 1: :
Fieldings Miscellanies 2 Vols :10:
Hales Discourses on the Common Prayer 4 Vols 2: :
Plinys Epistles 20/ Montaigns Essays 3 Vols £3 4: :
History of the present Parliament :10:
The History of Holland 2 Vols 20/ Whiston & Hare 5/ 1: 5:
[Tr]ial of Cyrus 1 Vol : 5:
Euclid's Elements 1st Volume 10/ :10:
Popes Works 3 Vols 20/ Hills Arithmetick 20/ 2: :
A New Methodical French Grammer : 5:
Gordons Geographical Grammer : 5:
Watts Miscellanies : 5:
Burnetts History of his own Times 6 Vols 3: :
Telemachus in French 20/ Doddridge on Religion 10/ 1:10:
The Revolutions of Portugal :15:

Title	Price
Senecas Morals 10/ Pomfrets Poems 10/	1: :
Jenks Devotions 10/ Paradise Lost 20/	1:10:
Moffets Health's Improvement	:10:
Clark on Study 10/ Ray on Creation 15/	1: 5:
Manners Translated from the French	:10:
The History of Charles the Twelfth King of Sweden	:15:
Sherlock on Death 5/ Landsdownes plays 10/	1: 5:
Watts Guide 10/ Harveys Meditations 2 Vols 40/	2:10:
Watts Guide to Prayer 5/ The Great Importance of a Religious Life 2/6 The Fable of the Bees 1st Vol 10/	:17: 6
The Guardian 2 Vols 5/ Le Theatre Italien 2 Vols 20/	1: 5:
The Jurisdiction of the House of Peers asserted	: 2: 6
An Essay towards an Instruction for Indians	: 2: 6
A Practical Treatise upon Cristian Perfection	:10:
A Methodical Treatise Concerning Bills of Exchange	: 5:
The Memoirs of an Ufortunate young Nobleman	:10:
Cato a Tragedy 5/ The Negociators Magazine 2/6	: 7: 6
Les Oeuvres De Moliere 4 Vols	1:10:
A French Bible 20/ A Common prayer Book in Latin 10/	1:10:
A Latin Bible 10/ Halifax's Miscellanies 15/	1: 5:
Tables for the Forbearance & discount of money	: 2: 6
The life & Death of John Earl of Rochester 2/6	: 2: 6
Memoirs of the House of Brandenburgh	:15:
A Short and Easy Method with the Deists & Jews	: 5:
Cassandra 4 Vols 40/ Popes Misscellanies 4 Vols 20/	3: :
L' Ecclesiaste De Solomon 5/ The adventures of Telemachus 2/6	: 7: 6
Sidney on poesy 5/ Memoirs of Major General Morgan 5/	:10:
Paradise Lost 20/ Congraves Plays 2 Vols 30/	2:10:

Item	Price
The Temple of Taste 5/ A Latin Grammer 2/6	: 7: 6
Huidibrass 2/6 A Compendium or Abreviation of Rights 2/6	: 5:
P. Ovidii Nasonis Opera 2/6 Swifts Works 9 Vols £ 5	5: 2: 6
Shakespears' Works 8 Vols £ 5 Tillotsons Works 10 Vols £ 5	10: :
Memoirs of Sir Charles Goodville & his family 2 Vols	1: :
The Adventurer Four Vols	2:10:
The supposed Daughter or Innocent Impostor 3 Vols	1:10:
A Poetical Translation of the Works of Horace 4 Vols	3: :
Joseph Addisons Miscellaneous Works 4 Vols	3: :
The Guardian 2 Vols 30/ The Tatler 4 Vols 60	4:10:
The Spectator 8 Vols £ 5 Cato's Letters 4 Vols £ 3	8: :
Clerk Sermons 11 Vols 70/ De Christo Imitando 2/6	3:12:6
A Discourse of Trade 2/6 Misscellaneous Poems 2/6	: 5:
A Common Prayer Book	:10:
The Doctrine of Interest both Simple & Compound	: 2: 6
Confession of Faith 5/ Parcel of Pamphlets £ 5	5: 5:
L'Escol Du Sage 2/6 The Histoy of King Henry the Great in french 5/	: 7: 6
The art of paintg in Oyl 2/6 a Common prayer Book in Latin 10/	:12: 6

JOHN MERCER[4]

Miscellanies

Title	Size	Price
Jacob's Collection of Heads for comonplacg	8o	: 1: 6
Chronica Juridicialia abridged	12o	: 4:
Naval Trade 2 vol	8o	:10:

[4]Manuscript Ledger, 1741–50, pp. 200–201, John Mercer Papers, Bucks County Historical Society, Doylestown, Pa. The verso of p. 200 is headed, "The Prices are the first Cost in Sterling money exclusive of Commission Shipping or other Charges."

G J Law & Lawyers laid open	8o	: 2: 6
Freeholders Companion	8o	: 5:
Law of Devises & Revocations	8o	: 3: 6
Puffendorf's Law of Nature & Nations	fol.	1: 8:
View of Civil & Ecclesiastical Law	12o	: 2: 6
Study & Body of the Law	12o	: 3:
Treatise of Bills of Exchange	12o	: 2: 6

Parliament

Cases in Parliament	fol.	:16:
Hunt's Postscript	8o	: 4:

Readings

Brooke's Reading on the Stat. of Limitacons	24o	: 1:

Reports

Alleyne's	fol.	: 9:
Anderson's	Do	1:15:
Barnardiston's	Do	1: 1:
Benloe's & Dalisons	Do	:10:
Bridgman's	Do	:18:
Bulstrode's	Do	4: 4:
Brownlow's & Goldesboroughs	4o	: 7:
Carter's	fol.	: 8:
Carthew's	Do	1: 2:
Cases in Chancery 3 Pts	Do	1:10:
Cases in BR & BC from 2d Wm 12 Mod	Do	1:10:
Cases in Law & Equity Macclesfield 10 Mod	Do	1: 4:
Coke's 11 Parts	Do	:15:
12 & 13 Parts	Do	: 7:
Comberbach's	Do	:17:
Croke's 3 vol.	Do	2:12: 6
Cary's	12o	: 3:
Clayton's	12o	: 3: 6
Davis's	fol.	:11:
Dyer's	Do	1:11: 6
Farraday's 7 Mod	Do	: 9:
Fitzgibbons's	Do	:14:

Gilbert's Repts in Equity & Exchegr	Do	:15:
Godbolt's	4o	1: 1:
Hardres's	fol	2:10:
Hatlay's	Do	:10:
Hobart's	Do	:16:
Holt's	Do	1:10:
Hutton's	Do	:13:
Jenkins's Centunies	Do	:16:
Jones's (Sr. Wm.)	Do	2: 5:
Jones's (Thos.)	Do	:15:
Keble's 3 vol.	Do	1:15:
Keilway's	Do	:14:
Kayling's	Do	: 9:
Lane's	Do	:16:
Latche's	Do	: 8:
Leonard's	Do	4: 4:
Levinz's 3 Parts 2 vol	Do	2: :
Ley's	Do	: 7:
Lilly's	Do	: 9:
Littleton's	Do	:11:
Lutwyche's 2 vol	Do	4: 4:
Modern Cases in Law & Equity 8 & 9 Mod	Do	1: 4:
Modern Reports 6 vol	Do	5: 5:
Moore's	Do	:18:
March's	4o	: 3:
Noy's	fol	:16:
Owen's	Do	:16:
Palmer's	Do	:12:
Plowden's	Do	2: 5:
Pollexfen's	Do	2: 2:
Popham's	Do	:14:
Precedents in Chancery	Do	1: 5:
Raymonds (Sr. Thos.)	Do	2:10:
Reports in Chancery in Finch's time	Do	:16:
Rolle's Reports	Do	2:10:
Reports in Chancery 4 vol	8o	:15:

Salkeld's 3 vol	fol	2:16:
Savile's	Do	: 6:
Saunders's	Do	1: 7: 6
Shower's 2 vol	Do	2: :
Select Cases in Com P. in Ld King's time	Do	: 8:
Siderfin's	Do	2: :
Skinner's	Do	1:10:
Styles's	Do	1:10:
Talbot's Cases in Equity	Do	:15:
Tothill's Transactions in Chancery	12o	: 1: 6
Vaughan's	fol	2:10:
Ventris's	Do	1:15:
Vernon's 2 vol	Do	2: 5:
Wynch's	Do	:16:
Williams's 2 vol	Do	2:16:
Year Books 9 vol	Do	3: 7: 6
Yelverton's	Do	: 5:
Zouch's Cases in the Civil Law	12o	: 2: 6
Cases in Chan & BR in Ld Hardwick's time	fol	:12:
Special & select Law Cases 1641	4o	: 5:

Sheriffs

Treatise of Replevins	8o	: 3:

Statutes

Keble's Statutes	fol	2:10:
Statutes concerning Bankrupts	12o	: 2: 6

Tables

Index to the Reports	fol	:15:

Abridgments

Cases in Equity abridged	fol	:18:
Danvers's Abridgment 3 vol	Do	3:10:
Viner's Abridgment 6 vol	Do	8: 8:
Davenport's Abridgmt of Coke on Littleton	12o	: 2:
Hughes's Abridgmt 2 vol	4o	:10:
Ireland's Abridgmt of Dyer's Reports	12o	: 2:

Rolle's Abridgmt interleaved 2 vol	fol	5: :
Salmon's Abridgmt of the State trials	Do	1:15:
Statutes abridged by Carey 2 vol	Do	2:10:
State trials abridged 1 vol	8o	: 5: 6
Virginia Laws abridged	8o	: 8:

Conveyancing

Ars Clericalis 1 vol	8o	: 4: 6
Compleat Conveyancer	8o	: 5:
Clerk's Guide	8o	: 5:
Clerk & Scriveners Guide	4o	: 8:
Herne's Law of Conveyances	8o	: 2:
Lawyer's Library	12o	: 3: 6
West's Symboleography	4o	: 5:

Courts & Courtkeeping

Attorneys Practise in CB	8o	: 6:
Attorney's Practise in BR 2 vol	8o	:12:
Coke's Institutes 4th Part	fol	:15:
R.R. Crown Circuit Companion	8o	: 6:
History of the Chancery	12o	: 2: 6
A.R.[5] Practise in Chancery 2 vol	12o	: 7:
Practick Part of the Law	8o	: 6:
G.J. Rules of Practise commonplaced	8o	: 4:
Practise of Chancery 1672	12o	: 1: 6
Harrisons Chancery Practiser	8o	: 6:

Crown

Coke's Institutes 3d Part	fol	:15:
Hale's History of the Pleas of the Crown 2 vol	Do	2:10:
Hawkin's Pleas of the Crown	Do	1:10:
Hale's Continuation of the Crown Law	8o	: 2: 6
Pulton de Pace Regis	fol	: 5:

[5]The initials "A.R.," "G.J.," "R.J." and "T.R." which appear next to certain titles probably indicate borrowers of those volumes.

Dictionaries

Cowell's Interpreter	fol	:10:
Jacob's Law Dictionary	Do	1: 8:
Law French Dictionary	8o	: 6:
R.J. Student's Law Dictionary	8o	: 5:
A.R. Terms de la Ley	8o	: 5:

Entries

Aston's	4o	: 3:
T.R. Brownlow's Declarations	4o	:12:
A.R. Bohun's Declarations	8o	: 6:
Brown's modus intrandi 2 vol	8o	:12:
Clift's	fol	1:10:
Coke's	Do	1: 1:
Lilly's	Do	1: 5:
Mallory's Quare Impedit	Do	:17:
Placita generalia & speciali	8o	: 3:
Rastall's	fol	1: 1:
Robinson's	Do	:10:
Read's Declarations	8o	: 3:
Vidian's	fol	:10:
Thompson's	Do	1: :

Justices of Peace

Justices vade mecum	12o	: 2:
Keble's Assistant to Justices	fol	: 5:
Manual for Justices 1641	12o	: 2:

Maxims

Doctor & Student	12o	: 3: 6
Finch's Law	12o	:14:
Francis's Maxims of Equity	fol	:18:
Hale's History & Analysis of the Laws	8o	: 6:
Hale's hereditary Descents	8o	: 1: 6
Hawke's Grounds of the Laws of England	12o	: 3:
Perkins's Law	12o	: 2: 6
Treatise of Equity	fol	: 8: 6
Woods Institutes of the Laws of England	Do	1: 5:

Miscellanies

Booth's real Actions	fol	: 8:
G.J. Baron & feme	8o	: 6:
Billinghurst of Bankrupts	12o	: 1: 6
Britton	12o	: 5:
Brown of fines & Recoveries	8o	: 5:
Coke's Institutes Comment on Littleton	fol	3: :
Part 2d	Do	1: 5:
G.J. Care's English Liberties	12o	: 2:
G.J. Curson's Law of Estates tail	8o	: 4: 6
Domat's Civil Law 2 vol	fol	2:10:
Dugdale's Origines Juridiciales	Do	2: :
Duncomb's Trials per pais 8o	8o	: 6:
Ejectments, Law of	8o	: 6:
G.J. Errors, Law of	8o	: 5:
G.J. Everyman his own Lawyer	8o	: 5:
Evidence Law of	8o	: 5:
G.J. Jacobs's Lex Mercatoria	8o	: 5:
G.J. Jus or Law of Masters & Servants	8o	: 3:
Landlord's Law	12o	: 3:
G.J. Law Quibbles	8o	: 4: 6
Laws of Liberty & Property	12o	: 2:
March's Actions for Slander & Arbitrations	8o	: 4:
Molloy de jure maritimo & navali	8o	: 7:
G.J. Obligations Law of	8o	: 5:
Sea Laws	4o	:12:
G.J. Treatise of Trover & Conversion	8o	: 2:
G.J. Trespasses (Law of) Vi & armis	8o	: 6:
Virginia Laws Purvis's[6]	fol	:12:
Virginia Laws by Parks 2 Vol	fol	2: :
Uses & Trusts (Law of	8o	: 6:
G.J. Usury (Law of	8o	: 2: 6
Freeholders Companion	8o	: 5:

[6]Purvis (and Parks in the following entry) were the publishers rather than the compilers of the Virginia statutes.

Tithes & Laws of the Clergy		
Hughes's Parson's Law	8o	: 1: 6
Wills Exrs &c		
Godolphin's Orphan's Legacy	4o	:12:
Meriton's Touchstone of Wills	12o	: 1: 6
A.R. Nelson's Lex Testamentaria	8o	: 7:
G.J. Swinburne of last Wills	4o	: 6:
Wentworth's Office of Executors	12o	: 2:
Writs		
A.R. Bohun's English Lawyer	8o	: 5:
Fitzherbert with Hale's Notes	4o	:16:
Fitzherbert's Natura Brevium	8o	: 6:
Registrum Brevium	fol	1: 1:
Omitted		
Laws of Maryland	fol	1: :
Statutes of Excise	12o	: 1: 6

BENET OLDHAM[7]

Kebles Statutes £10 Cooks £15	25: :
Cookes Institutes & Upon Littleton £10 Livints reports £7	17: :
Hawkins Pleas of the Crown £7 Sinderfins reports £3	10: :
Woods Institutes £7 Fortisquis Laws £5	12: :
Ditto in Parliament Cases	3: :
Jacobs Law Dictionary £5 Blunts Law Dictionary 50/	7:10:
Spealmans Closerium 40/ Tables of reports of all Cases 40/	4: :
Trotts Laws £5 Bracton on the Law 40/	7: :
Wingates maxum of the Law 20/ Virgils works 10/	1:10:
Parson on the Creed 7/6 Juvinals Satire 10/	1: 7: 6

[7]Inventories X, pp. 407–408, South Carolina Department of Archives and History, Columbia, S.C. The values are in South Carolina currency.

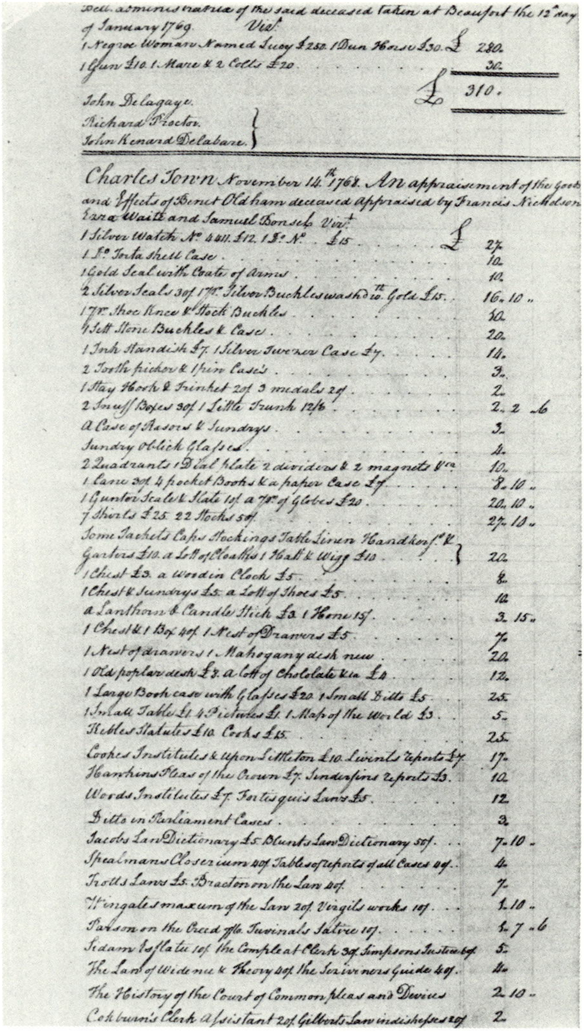

...administratrix of the said deceased taken at Beaufort the 12th day of January 1769. Viz[t]

	£
1 Negroe Woman Named Lucy £250. 1 Dun Horse £30.	280.
1 Gun £10. 1 Mare & 2 Colts £20.	30.
	£ 310.

John Delagaye.
Richard Proctor.
John Kenard Delabare.

Charles Town November 14th 1768. An appraisement of the Goods and Effects of Benet Oldham deceased Appraised by Francis Nicholson Ezra Waite and Samuel Bonsell Viz[t]

	£		
1 Silver Watch No 4411. £12. 1 D[o] No £15	27.		
1 D[o] Torta shell Case	10.		
1 Gold Seal with Coate of Arms	10.		
2 Silver Seals 30/ 1 P[r] Silver Buckles wash'd wth Gold £15.	16.	10.	
1 P[r] Shoe Knee & Stock Buckles	10.		
4 Sett Stone Buckles & Case	20.		
1 Ink Standish £7. 1 Silver Tweezer Case £7.	14.		
2 Tooth pickers & 1 pin Cases	3.		
1 Stay Hook & Trinket 20/ 3 medals 20/	2.		
2 Snuff Boxes 30/ 1 Little Trunk 12/6	2.	2	6
A Case of Rasors & Sundrys	3.		
Sundry Oblick Glasses	4.		
2 Quadrants 1 Dial plate 2 dividers & 2 magnets &c[a]	10.		
1 Cane 30/ 4 pocket Books & a paper Case £7	8.	10.	
1 Gunter Scale & Slate 10/ a P[r] of Globes £20	20.	10.	
7 Shirts £25. 22 Stocks 50/	27.	10.	
Some Jackets Caps Stockings Table Linen Handkerf.[s] & Garters £10. a Lott of Cloaths 1 Hatt & Wigg £10	20.		
1 Chest £3. a Wooden Clock £5.	8.		
1 Chest & Sundrys £5. a Lott of Shoes £5.	10.		
a Lanthorn & Candle Stick £3. 1 Hone 15/	3.	15.	
1 Chest & 1 Box 40/ 1 Nest of Drawers £5.	7.		
1 Nest of drawers 1 Mahogany desk new	20.		
1 Old poplar desk £8. a Lott of Chocolate &c[a] £4.	12.		
1 Large Book case with Glasses £20. 1 Small Ditto £5.	25.		
1 Small Table £1. 4 Pictures £1. 1 Map of the World £3.	5.		
Keebles Statutes £10. Cooks £15.	25.		
Cookes Institutes & upon Littleton £10. Lewints Reports £7.	17.		
Hawkins Pleas of the Crown £7. Sundersons Reports £3.	10.		
Woods Institutes £7. Fortesquis Laws £5.	12.		
Ditto in Parliament Cases	3.		
Jacobs Law Dictionary £5. Blunts Law Dictionary 50/.	7.	10.	
Spealmans Closerium 40/ Tables of reports of all Cases 40/.	4.		
Trotts Laws £5. Bracton on the Law 40/.	7.		
Wingates maxum of the Law 20/. Virgils works 10/.	1.	10.	
Parson on the Creed of the Juvinals Satire 10/.	1.	7.	6
Sidams Is Platu 10/. the Compleat Clerk 30/. Simpsons Justice 60/.	5.		
The Law of Widence & Theory 40/. the Scriveners Guide 40/.	4.		
The History of the Court of Common pleas and Devices	2.	10.	
Cokburn's Clerk Assistant 20/. Gilberts Law in dishepses 20/	2.		

Estate Inventory of Benet Oldham.
South Carolina Department of Archives and History, Columbia.

Sidam Estates 10/ the Compleat Clerk 30/ Simpsons Justice 60/	5: :
The Law of evidence & Theory 40/ the Scriviners Guide 40/	4: :
The History of the Court of Common pleas and Devises	2:10:
Cokburn's Clerk Assistant 20/ Gilberts Law in distresses 20/	2: :
Floyers Practice 20/ the Lawyer of Attorneys &ca 10/	1:10:
Cuhuns Institution 20/ Harrisons Practice in Chancery 30/	2:10:
The Law of Exors & admors 10/ Jacobs Statutes Table 10/	1: :
Tuncum Tryells of Race 10/ The Law interpreter 5/	:15:
Blacksons In Alleces 15/ Institutes of Impr Law 7/6	1: 2: 6
Law Lowdger 10/ Rules & Orders of Kings Bench 15/	1: 5:
Law of Infants 10/ Perrys Law 10/ Doctr & Studants 20/	2: :
Attys Practice Kings Bench 2 Vols Do of the Common pleas	2: :
Hurbert 10/ History of Common Law 10/ Practice of Trover & ca 5/	1: 5:
French Dictionary 20/ Common Law 10/ Stanfords pleas 20/	2:10:
Law Dictionary 20/ Crocks reports 5/ Actions on y case 5/	1:10:
Wise on Civil Law 5/ Atty pocket Companion 2 Vols 30/	1:15:
Tenants Law 10/ Turys Dictionary on admiralty Souts Do 15/	1: 5:
Jacobs Law Grammer 5/ discourse on Law Terms 2/6	: 7: 6
Finil discourse on Law Lyttleton Do	:10:
A Small Latin Book 2/6 Justice Incairls Institutions 5/	: 7: 6
Law of Nature & Nations	: 5:
A Guide to the Rights of Englishmen 5/ English Libertyes 5/	:10:
A Guide to the Knowledge of English Libertys	: 5:

Peptuagin 40/ Popes works 9 Vols £9	11: :
Swifts works £10. 3 old Rush Botton Chairs 20/	11: :

PETER LEIGH[8]

Andersons Reports	1:10:
Bacons Abridgment 3 Vols	20: :
Bridgemans Conveyances	7: :
Browns Entries Latin	:10:
Cookes 1,2,3, & 4 Institutes	20: :
Cokes Reports French 2 Vols folio	2: :
Ditto English	3: :
Cases Equity abridged	4: :
Cases in Parliament	2: :
Davy's Reports	: 5:
Danver's Abridgement 3 Vols	20: :
Dyers Reports	1:10:
Farresleys Reports	3: :
Hardress Ditto	7: :
Hawkins Pleas of the Crown	7: :
Hales Ditto	10: :
Hobarts Reports	3: :
Jones Sr. Thomas Reports	1:10:
Ditto Sr. William Ditto	1:10:
Levinz Reports French 3 Vols	3: :
Levinz Entries Ditto	:10:
Lutwiches Reports Ditto 2 Vols	3: :
Moores Reports	1:10:
Maxims in Equity	1:10:
Nelsons Abridgement 3 Vols	5: :
Peere Williams Rep[or]t[s] [3][9] Ditto	15: :
Quare impedit	: 5:
Rules Common ple[as] [ ]	4: :
Styles Reports	3: :
Sheppards Actions o[n Case]	1: :
Statutes at Large [Vols]	70: :
State Tryals 8 Ditto [ ]	70: :
Salkelds Reports 3[Vols]	7: :
Viners Abridgment [ ]	6: :
Ventris Reports 2[Vols]	5: :

[8]Inventories T, pp. 256–57, South Carolina Department of Archives and History, Columbia, S.C. The values are in South Carolina currency.

[9]The manuscript is torn from this entry to that for Jenkins's Reports.

Title	Price
Hawkins Pleas of [the Crown] [ ]dged	1:15:
Law of Ejectment [ ]	1: 5:
Wrights Tenur[es]	:10:
Fortescue de Leg[ibus]	2: :
Jenkins Reports	1:10:
Brooks Abridgment	1:10:
Trotts Collection of Carolina Laws	12: :
Fitzherberts new Nat Brevium	3: :
Waterhouse on [Fortes]ue[10]	2: :
Law of Evide[nce]	1: 5:
Jacob Statute [-Law Com]mon Pl	1: :

Title	Price
Bohuns Law of T[ithes] Doctrine [of Demur]rers Perfect Con[ve]yancer, Entering Clerks vade mecum Infants Lawyer [Laws for] and against Bankrupts [ ]matts Treatise on fines [ ] Law in General J[ ] Abr Statutes [ ] Jurisdi[ ]	
Cokes En[tries]	1:10:
Dr. Lodge [ ]	2: :
Rastells En[tries]	1:10:
Rastells Tables	: 5:
1 Large Abridgment	1: :

[10]The manuscript is torn or obliterated by discoloration from this entry to that for Rastell's Tables.

INDEX

The arrangement of works alphabetically by authors' names and the separate alphabetical listing of library owners preclude the need to include authors or library owners in this index, except as they appear in the introductory materials and deserve some special notice. On the other hand this index does contain titles; many of these are cited without reference to their authors and many have commonly used short titles, which are also indexed here. The Table of Titles in the Appendix is arranged by legal classifications, thus permitting the reader to survey imprints in a given field without recourse to an index.

Abridgment of Cases in Equity, 23
An Abridgment of the Common Law, 41
An Abridgment of the First Part of my Lord Coke's Institutes, 29
Abridgments, xiii
The Accomplish'd Practiser in the High court of chancery, 29
Acquisition of books
  availability and, ix–x
  bookseller's advertisements and, xxxv
  reception of law and, xii–xiii
  utility and, ix
Adams, John
  book acquisitions of, xxv
Admiralty jurisdiction, xix–xx, xxii–xxiii
American imprints, x
An Analysis of the Laws . . ., 6
The Attorney's Pocket Companion, 39–40
The Attorney's Practice in the Court of Common Pleas: . . ., 48
The Attorney's Practice in the Court of King's Bench . . ., 48
The Attorney's Vade Mecum, and Client's Instructor, 41
The Authority, Jurisdiction and Method of Keeping County-courts, . . ., 26

Bail in Civil and Criminal Cases, 30
Bankrupt Laws, 15
Baron and Feme, 4–5
Bibliotheca Legum: . . ., 58
Bibliotheca Legum Angliae, 58 n.73
Bills of Exchange, 35

Blackstone, Sir William
Commentaries, xiv
Book of Oaths . . ., 8
Bookseller's advertisements, xxxv
Bridgman's Conveyances, 9
A Brief Disquisition on the Law of Nature, . . ., 53
Burn, Richard, xvii

Carter, Samuel, 37 n.50
Cases in Law: Wherein Justices of the Peace have a Jurisdiction, 6
Catalogue of the Common and Statute Law Books . . ., 5
Chancery jurisdiction, xvii–xix
Choice Presidents upon all Acts of Parliament Relating to . . . a Justice of the Peace, 35
The Civil Law in its Natural Order: . . ., 18–19
The Clergy-Man's Law: . . ., 55
Clerke, Francis
The Practice of the Court of Admiralty . . ., xix–xx
Clerk's Assistant in the Practice of the Ecclesiastical Courts, 13
Clerk's Manual, . . ., 12
Clerk's Tutor in Chancery, . . ., 9
Codex Juris Ecclesiastici Anglicani: . . ., 24
Collecteana Juridica; . . ., 28
A Collection of Modern Entries, . . ., 38
A Collection of Select and Modern Entries . . ., 37–38
A Collection of tracts relative to the Law of England, 28–29
Commentaries, xiii
Commentaries on the Laws of England, 6
The Commentaries or Reports of Edmund Plowden, 44
Commercial law; *see* Law merchant
The Common Law Common-placed, 32
Common law practice, xvii
A Compendious and Accurate Treatise of Fines upon writs of covenant; . . ., 9–10
A Compendious System of the Bankrupt Laws, 15
The Compleat Arbitrator: . . ., 3
The Compleat Clerk in Court; . . ., 14
The Compleat Sheriff: . . ., 14
A Complete body of Conveyancing, . . ., 56
A Complete Digest of . . . Insurance, 56
The Constitution of England, 39
A Continuation of the Practical Register, . . ., 38
Conveyancing, xxi–xxii
Conveyancing manuals, xiii
The Country Justice, 17
County Judicatures, 26
Criminal law, xxii
The Crown Circuit Companion, 51
Crown Law, 21
Cumberland, Richard, 53
Cursus Cancellariae: . . ., 7

Dana, Francis
library list of, 66–67
De Jure Belli Ac Pacis . . ., 27
De Jure Maritimo et Navali: . . ., 40–41
De laudibus legum Angliae, 20
De Officio Hominis & Civis juxta Legem Naturalem, 46
De Successionibus apud Anglos: The Law of Hereditary Descents, 27
Debt collection, xvii
Declarations and Pleadings in the most usual Actions . . ., 7–8
A Defense of the Constitutions of Government, 3

Dictionaries, law, xiii
A Digest of the Doctrine of Bail, 30
A Digest of the Laws of England, 14
Digesti Justiniani Institutionum . . ., 18
A Discourse concerning Inheritances in fee simple . . ., 48–49
Doctor and Student: . . ., 50
The Doctrine of Demurrers, . . ., 21
Duncombe, Giles
  Tryals per pais, xxii

Ecclesiastical Law, 11
Eighteenth-century imprints, short-title
  bibliography of, xi
Elements of the Civil Law, 52
Elements of the Law relating to Insurances, 40
English law, reception of, xii
The English Lawyer: showing the nature, forms of original writs, . . ., 8
English Liberties: . . ., 12
The English Pleader, . . ., 9
English Reports, Full Reprint, xi
The English Works of Sir Henry Spelman . . ., 51
An Enquiry into the Foundation . . . *of the Law of Nations,* 55
The Entring Clerk's Introduction, 10
An Essay on . . . *the Creation and Execution of Powers,* 44
An Essay on the Law of Bailments, 34
An Essay on the Learning of Contingent Remainders and Executory Devises, 18
An Essay upon . . . *Devises,* 45
Essay upon British Antiquities, 34
Essay upon the Law of Contracts . . ., 45
Essays upon Several Subjects concerning British antiquities, 34
Every Man his own Lawyer; . . ., 32
An Exact Abridgment of all the Statutes . . . (Washington), 55
An Exact Abridgment of all the Statutes . . . (Wingate), 56
The Exact Pleader, 54

Fines and Recoveries, Treatise of, 9–10
The First Part of the Institutes of the Laws of England, 13–14
Formularies, xiii

A General Abridgment of Cases in Equity, . . ., 23
A General Abridgment of the Common Law, . . ., 17–18
A General Abridgment of Law and Equity, . . ., 54–55
A General Treatise of the Dominion and Laws of the Sea, 34
A General Treatise of Naval Trade and Commerce, . . ., 23–24
Grindlay, James
  estate inventory of, 67–76

Historia Placitorum Coronae. The History of the Pleas of the Crown . . ., 28
Historical Law-tracts, 34
The History and Analysis of the Common Law of England; . . ., 27–28
The History and Practice of the Court of Common Pleas, 24
History of the English law . . ., 47–48
The History of the Chancery; . . ., 12
The History of the Common Law, 27–28
History of Common Pleas, 24

Infant's Lawyer, 31
An Institute of the Laws of England;..., 56–57
Institutes; *see* Commentaries
Institutes of Natural Law;..., 49
Institutio Legalis:..., 8
Institutions de Droit de la Nature et des Gens..., 56
Instructor Clericalis, 21–23
The Interpreter, 15–16
Introduction to the Law of Tenures..., 58
An Introduction to the Law Relative to Trials at Nisi Pruis, 11

Jacob, Giles
  Every man his own lawyer, xiv
  Lex Mercatoria, xxii
James, Eldon R.
  list of American law treatises, x
Jefferson, Thomas, xxv
Jus Imperii & Servitutis, 34
Justice of the Peace, 35
The Justice of the Peace and Parish Officer, 11
Justice of the Peace manuals, xvi–xvii
Justinian's Institutes, 18

The Law Against Bankrupts, 26
The Law Concerning Estates Taile,..., 17
The Law-dictionary:..., 33 n.45
A Law-dictionary and Glossary, 7
A Law Dictionary; The Interpreter..., 15–16
The Law Dictionary, Interpreting..., 7
The Law-French Dictionary alphabetically digested, 37
Law Grammar, 32
Law merchant, xxii–xxiii
The Law of Actions on the Case for Torts and Wrongs, 35
Law of Bailments, 34
The Law of Bill of Exchange,..., 16
The Law of Commons and Commoners;..., 35–36
The Law of Corporations, 36
The Law of Covenants;..., 36
The Law of Devises, Revocations and Last Wills, 24
The Law of Distresses and Replevins delineated, 24–25
The Law of Ejectments,..., xxi, 36
The Law of Errors and Writs of Error, 36
The Law of Evidence, 25, 41
The Law of Executions:..., 37
The Law of Executors and Administrators, 37
The Law of Inheritances in Fee,..., 48–49
Law of Insurances, 40
Law of Masters and Servants, 34
The Law of Mortgages, 12
The Law of Nations:..., 54
The Law of Uses and Trusts:..., 25
Law, or, A discourse thereof:..., 19
Law Quibbles, 32
Law Tracts (Bacon), 3
Law Tracts (Blackstone), 7
The Laws of England Delineated, 37
Laws of the Sea, 34
Laws Relating to the Poor..., 20
Lawyers' libraries, ix
Le Droit de la nature et des gens..., 46
Legal education
  books in, xiii–xiv
  broad definition of, in eighteenth century, xxiv–xxv
  Inns of Court as a mode of, xxv–xxvi
  Liberal arts and, xxiii–xxiv
Legal history, xxiii

Leigh, Peter
estate inventory of, 86–87
Les Terms de la Ley, 47
Lex Mercatoria; . . ., 32
Lex Mercatoria Rediviva: . . ., 5
Lex Testamentaria, 42
Lex Vadiorum, 12
Libraries, extant, xxx–xxxii
Lists, library, xxxii–xxxv
Littleton, A Commentary upon, 13–14

Maxims and Rules of Pleading . . ., 30
Maxims of Equity, . . ., 20
Mercer, John
library list of, 76–83
A Methodical System of Universal Law: . . ., 30
Mirrour of Justices, 31
Modern Conveyancer, 40
Modern Entries, 37–38
Modern Entries, in English, 40
The Modern Practice of . . . Chancery, 30
Modus Intrandi placita generalia: . . ., 10
Molloy, Charles
De Jure Maritimo, xxii

The Nature and Practice of Real Actions . . ., 9
A New Abridgment . . ., 3–4
A New Abridgment and Critical Review of the State Trials, . . ., 50
A New and Complete law-dictionary, . . ., 17
The New Instructor Clericalis, 31
A New Institute of the Imperial, or Civil Law, 57
A New Law-dictionary: . . ., 33
The New Law of Evidence, 25
The new Natura brevium . . ., 20
New Precedents in Conveyancing, 43
Notes of Cases in Points of Practice: . . ., 4

Observations on the more ancient statutes, 5 n.6
Observations upon the statutes, . . ., 5
Of Last Wills and Testaments, 43
Of the Law of Nature and Nations, 46
Of the Rights of War and Peace: . . ., 27
The Office and Authority of a Justice of the Peace, 42
The Office and Duty of Executors: . . ., 55–56
Office of an Attorney, 23
Office of Sheriffs, 17
Officium Clerici Pacis, 43
Officium Vicecomitum, 17
Old Law of Evidence, 41
Oldham, Benet
estate inventory of, 83–86
Opera Omnia, 50
Opera omnia juridica, 42
The Origin of Laws, Arts and Sciences, . . ., 26
The Orphan's Legacy, 26

Placita Coronae, 53
Pleader's Assistant, 44
Pleas of the Crown; . . . (Hale), 28
Pleas of the Crown (Tremaine), 53
The Pocket Conveyancer, 44
The Practical Conveyancer, 38
A practical demonstration of county-judicatures, 26
The Practical Register (134 Lilly), 38
The Practical Register: . . . (136 Lilly), 38–39
The Practical Register in Chancery: . . ., 45
Practice common-placed; . . ., 16

Practice manuals, xiii
The Practice of Courts-Leet and Courts-Baron, 50
The Practice of the Court of Admiralty of England, 13
The Practice of the Spiritual or Ecclesiastical Courts, 15
Practicer in Chancery, 29
The Practick Part of the Law:..., 23
Praxis Almae Curiae Cancellariae:..., 10
Praxis Curiae admiralitatis angliae, 13 n.19
Precedents in Chancery,..., 45–46
Precedents in Conveyancing, 31
A Preparative to Pleading, 53
Principles of Equity, 35
Privilegia Londini:..., 8
Probate jurisdiction, xx–xxi
Proceedings in Chancery; see Cursus Cancellariae
The Proctor's Practice in the Ecclesiastical Courts, 20
Pufendorf, Samuel Baron von, xxiv

Quare Impedit, 40

Readings upon the Statute Law, 47
Real property, xvii, xxi n.17
Redesdale, John Freeman-Mitford, Baron
  A Treatise of the Pleadings ... in Chancery, xiv
A Report of some Proceedings ... for the Trial of the Rebels in the year 1746, 21
Reports of cases, xi
A review of the statutes,..., 33 n.47
Rules and Orders of the Court of Chancery..., 49
The Scrivener's Guide, 15
Some Considerations on the Law of Forfeitures for High Treason, 58
The Statute-law Common-plac'd:..., 33
Statutues, xii
The Statutes at Large concerning Bankrupts..., 51
A System of Pleading,..., 50
A System of the Law of Marine Insurances, 43
A Systematic View of the Laws of England, 57

Table of Precedents, 15
Table to the Statutes, 33
Tables to the Modern Printed Presidents..., 15
Tenants Law:..., 52
Terms de la Ley, 47
The Touch-Stone of Common Assurances..., 51
Trade patterns, xvi
A Treatise concerning Trespasses Vi et Armis, 12
A Treatise of Common Recoveries, 43
A Treatise of Distresses, Replevins and Avowries,..., 53
A Treatise of Equity, 4
A Treatise of Frauds, Covins and Collusions..., 53
A Treatise of Law and Equity, Concerning Husbands and Wives..., 4 n.5
A Treatise of the Pleas of the Crown:..., 29–30
A Treatise of Tenures, 25
A Treatise of Testaments and Last Wills,..., 52
A Treatise of the Laws of Nature, 16
A Treatise of the Pleadings in Suits ... by English Bill, 47

Index

A Treatise on the Law of Bills of Exchange and Promissory Notes, 35
A Treatise upon the Law of Mortgages, 45
Trespasses Vi et Armis, 12
The Trial of Dr. Henry Sacheverell . . ., 49
The Trial of Thomas Earl of Macclesfield, 39
Trials at Nisi Prius, 11
Trials per pais: . . ., 19

Vade Mecum, 41

Imported Eighteenth-Century Law Treatises in American Libraries, 1700–1799, has been composed in Compugraphic Bembo. Michelangelo and Centaur Italic were selected for display. The book was designed by Jim Billingsley, typeset by Metricomp, Inc., printed by offset lithography by Thomson-Shore, Inc., and bound by John H. Dekker and Sons.

THE UNIVERSITY OF TENNESSEE PRESS : KNOXVILLE